DOn't QuIT

The Jason Merkle Story

KYLE S. REYNOLDS

WESTBOW
PRESS®
A DIVISION OF THOMAS NELSON
& ZONDERVAN

This book is a work of non-fiction. Unless otherwise noted, the author and the publisher make no explicit guarantees as to the accuracy of the information contained in this book and in some cases, names of people and places have been altered to protect their privacy.

WestBow Press books may be ordered through booksellers or by contacting:

WestBow Press
A Division of Thomas Nelson & Zondervan
1663 Liberty Drive
Bloomington, IN 47403
www.westbowpress.com
1 (866) 928-1240

Scripture quotations are from The ESV® Bible (The Holy Bible, English Standard Version®), copyright © 2001 by Crossway, a publishing ministry of Good News Publishers. Used by permission. All rights reserved.

ISBN: 978-1-9736-6895-4 (sc)
ISBN: 978-1-9736-6896-1 (hc)
ISBN: 978-1-9736-6894-7 (e)

Library of Congress Control Number: 2019909923

Print information available on the last page.

WestBow Press rev. date: 08/20/2019

From Jason

For Jay and Patty Merkle
No words can suffice to offer the appreciation that Jason's parents
deserve for their around-the-clock care of Jason during the most
harrowing battle of his life. The love and service they offered Jason
mirrored that of God's immense, limitless love of his own children.
We should all hope to exhibit the same vast, unconditional love
for our own children during the inevitable tribulations of life.

and

For Kristen Merkle
You revive me and sustain me. Life is so
wonderful with you by my side.

From Kyle

For Catherine
You have believed in me from the beginning,
and you are the love of my life.

and

For my late mother
You always had big dreams for me, and
I am living them out for you.

Contents

Introduction

"Wake up, Jason! Wake up!" Water was repeatedly sprayed onto my face, and I was incessantly slapped like a child who had misbehaved. This went on for several minutes, according to my dad, as I lay there like a dead man, unresponsive and unmoving. Both my parents participated in the ordeal, slapping and spraying, spraying and slapping until I woke up from my virtually impenetrable slumber. As bad as this experience was, this occurred every two hours all night long, every night, for nearly six months. It was 2001, just a few weeks after the catastrophic 9/11 attack on the United States, and at this point, I was just a few months into the fight of my life. The doctors had recently shared a grim diagnosis that had shaken my family to its core—I was only twenty years old. Each time I regained consciousness from this insane and exhausting wake-up party, I felt like I had been hit by an eighteen-wheeler. My face was swollen from the steroids the doctors had prescribed, and my eyesight was extremely poor due to the tumor's pervasion of my brain. What's more, I experienced a constant ringing in my ears caused by the steroids. Frankly, I looked like a blind, half-deaf Pillsbury Doughboy. Still, I was optimistic that things might get better, but for now, the task at hand was simply to use the bathroom. If I didn't use the bathroom every couple of hours, I would likely wet the bed due to my excessive water intake.

It was a humiliating and daunting time, being sprayed and slapped until I finally woke up to use the bathroom. It was a test of patience and faith for sure, and I knew that I had to endure. Having just been diagnosed with terminal brain cancer, I had rejected the conventional, mainstream treatments, such as chemotherapy, radiation, and surgery. And things were bad—really bad, in fact. People use the expression "sicker than a dog," but I was sicker than a shipwrecked sailor, seasick and nearly drowned in a storm. Had we made the right decision in rejecting conventional treatment? To look at me then one might say we were idiots for not listening to the doctors.

Every day was a battle in and of itself during this early season in my war against cancer. I had begun the alternative treatment on August 1—it was an ingenious approach to fighting cancer, at least on paper. My parents and I were given proof that this approach could work through the long list of other survivors provided by this alternative clinic. Knowing that this was clearly a life-or-death situation, my parents were relentless in pushing me through each of the six treatments a day. I was bound and determined to fight this awful disease and never give up. "DOn't quIT" became my daily mantra, and my faith in God and reliance upon him and him alone would be the rock I could stand on during this perilous battle ahead. Psalm 18:2 states, "The Lord is my rock and my fortress and my deliverer, my God, my rock in whom I take refuge, my shield, and the horn of my salvation, my stronghold." From a very young age, I had memorized this verse, and I treasured it in my heart during this time.

What follows is the story about the fight of my life, a harrowing period of hand-to-hand combat with the cancerous foe inside my head, as told by my friend and author, Kyle Steven Reynolds. He has helped me recreate the smaller stories inside the larger one that detail some of the people and events that were a part of this journey. Some names have been changed or excluded altogether for safety and privacy reasons. May God bless you as he has blessed me, and it is my hope that this story will help strengthen your resolve to never give up and always keep fighting, even when things could not seem worse.

Prologue

Cast your cares on the Lord and he will sustain you;
he will never let the righteous fall.

—Psalm 55:22

Why is quitting such an epidemic in today's world? Why do people quit, give up, and lose confidence in their abilities?

Stories about quitters are rarely told because they are all too common and discouraging. People want to hear about heroes, not the rampant throes of failures. With the exception of the jaded few, people want to read about men or women who, against all odds, toppled their own fear and anxieties and overcame extreme and overwhelming obstacles. But how many of us shrink in the face of those obstacles, turn the other direction, and trudge down the path well-trodden, or the easy way?

The story of Jason Merkle is not just a story about one young man's fight against cancer; it is a story about having faith that God has equipped human beings with the strength to conquer all nemeses and obliterate all fears. Jason was fortunate enough to grow up in a home with strong Christian parents who instilled in their boys the importance and effectiveness of faith and prayer. In the Merkle household, God was not some far-off divine being who was disinterested in the lives of humans—he was a permeating, omnipresent, and life-giving force who loves human beings beyond comprehension, despite the sinful human heart.

Why then does an all-loving God with the power to eliminate all pain and disease permit such horrendous suffering, especially among innocent children? In this book, we will tackle this formidable and unique human question. The short answer to this question is that there is no easy answer, but the Bible makes clear that no one, male or female, is innocent before God. The tragic story of humankind's great fall away from God is chronicled in Genesis, the first book of the Bible. God gave commands to his creation to abide in him and thus live in prosperity and peace. Humans, thinking they knew better, succumbed to the temptation of the serpent, thus plunging creation into the despair of a sinful existence, where a new and unbridgeable chasm now existed between a Holy God and evil humanity. In fact, God told Adam and Eve that they had brought suffering and even death upon themselves in disobeying him:

> Cursed is the ground because of you; through painful toil you will eat of it all the days of your life. It will produce thorns and thistles for you, and you will eat the plants of the field. By the sweat of your brow you will eat your food until you return to the ground, since from it you were taken; for dust you are and to dust you will return. (Gen. 3:17–19)

It is in this passage that God formally declares humankind's entrance into a dark reality—one in which they are no longer protected from evil by the walls of Paradise, but rather they have stepped out willingly onto a grand battlefield in which absolute evil is in constant opposition to God's eternal will. What's remarkable in this is not that God exhibits his wrath against humankind, which was actually a righteous and just action, but instead that in spite of this malicious disobedience against the Father, God still furnishes a path back into his presence through the life, death, and resurrection of Jesus Christ. The remainder of the Bible can be summed up succinctly as God implementing a divine plan in which he most lovingly seeks after his people, working to redeem their lives from the pit. In essence, God tirelessly pursues his creation even to the point of sacrificing his one and only Son on the cross in order to wipe out all transgressions for eternity. "Greater love has no one than this, that he lay down his life for his friends" (John 15:13).

In the story that follows, Jason Merkle demonstrated a profound faith in God at just twenty years of age. God gifted him with the faith and determination to battle the cancer that he was predestined to fight. And ultimately, through faith in Jesus Christ, there are no failures, only victors.

Chapter 1

The Throes of Childhood

Jason Merkle was born on February 19, 1981. He was the third boy born in a family of five boys, a family brimming with testosterone. His first name, Jason, is derived from the Greek word, Ἰάσων (*Iasōn*), which means "healer" or "one that will heal." Much of Jason's life serves as a testament for his given name bestowed upon him by his parents, Jay and Patty Merkle.

For the first thirteen years of Jason's life, he lived a relatively normal, yet active, existence. He grew up in a middle-class home in Williamston, Michigan; attended church each and every Sunday; played soccer, football, and baseball; and attended public school alongside his four brothers—Matthew, Daniel, Jonathan, and Jordan. Jason's early life resembled that of a typical middle-class American boy extolling the masculine virtues of athleticism, strength, confidence, and ambition. More importantly, though, from a very young age, Jason learned to praise God for all the blessings he received and the gifts he exhibited. There was no shortage of prayer in the Merkle household— it was a daily routine impressed upon Jason by his parents, who taught him from a very early age that prayer was important, whether things are good or bad in one's life. In this way, seeking out God meant not just calling upon the Lord in times of need or struggle but calling out to him on a daily basis in a tone of worship.

Life in Williamston was simple—very simple. Located just fifteen miles southeast of East Lansing and seventy-five miles northwest of Detroit, Jason grew up in a quiet community of around three thousand people. Named after James Williamston, who became the town's first mayor in 1871, the Williamston area had previously been settled by a small band of Chippewa Indians, with Chief Okemos (meaning "Little Chief") as the most notable figurehead of the group. Chief Okemos once boasted a five-inch scar on the left side of his forehead, acquired in battle with the American cavalry; a saber had slashed his head open while he was fighting alongside the British in the War of 1812. Scars, while resulting often from painful injury or circumstance, often become bragging rights later in life, which was certainly the case for Chief Okemos. Little did he know, but Jason would join Chief Okemos as having cause to boast about scars in the early years of his life.

In 1994, when Jason was just thirteen years old, his relatively quiet life changed drastically. Jason was just in the seventh grade, and his parents noticed that his grades began to slip, and worse, he began experiencing noticeable tremors in his hands. At first, Jason and his parents did not become overly alarmed, as Jason was still a very active child who, like all thirteen-year-old boys, was experiencing the onslaught of adolescence. After all, many kids experience dramatic changes in their bodies during this time, and all teenagers experience at least moderate anxiety as their bodies develop and change.

Van Merkle, Jason's uncle and esteemed chiropractor and nutritionist, first noticed Jason's tremors during a Fourth of July weekend in Dayton, Ohio. Van had taught all of the Merkle boys to ski; each one was water skiing by the time he was six years old. While Jason was an experienced water skier, Van noticed that he was having an extremely difficult time getting up and staying up on his skis. Normally, an experienced water-skier like Jason would have no trouble balancing on his skis after a couple of attempts, but suddenly Jason was struggling mightily. After Jason came out of the water, Van noticed that he was shaking. Van asked Jason's brothers about whether they had seen him shake like this before, and they just shrugged it off, saying, "He just shakes like Grandpa sometimes." Originally, Van thought the shaking might just be a fluke—maybe Jason was ill, possibly cold, or just tired. But now Van, knowing what he knew about the human body, thought this could possibly be a blood-sugar issue or even a problem with Jason's brain. He gave Jason something to eat, but Jason could not stop shaking long enough to get the food into his mouth. Van began to panic. Something was seriously wrong.

Van informed his brother, Jay, and his sister-in-law, Patty, that they needed to take Jason in for a CT scan immediately. Later that week, heeding Van's advice, they took Jason in to get the scan. Jason's family doctor referred Jason to a specialist, who discovered that there was extra fluid on his brain. With a lackadaisical approach, which Jason's mother shall never forget, the specialist pointed out that this excess fluid could develop into a more serious issue but said that they would further investigate after he came back from vacation.

Jason's mother, appalled by the doctor's cool indifference to the immediacy of the situation, reacted as any concerned, conscientious mother would—she took Jason immediately to the hospital to have an MRI performed. When they arrived at the hospital, the nurses were reluctant to give Jason an MRI since no doctor had referred him to the hospital, not to mention the fact that MRIs were extremely expensive. Jason's mother, however, sensing the urgency of the matter, demanded that an MRI be performed right away. The importance of this moment cannot be understated—without a doctor's orders, having an MRI performed at the hospital was simply unfathomable. No neurologist had ordered the MRI, and yet here were a mother and son insisting that the expensive procedure be done anyway. An MRI (or Magnetic Resonance Image) is a cost-prohibitive procedure that is normally done only after extensive CT scan analysis, and some insurance companies would not even cover the cost of an MRI unless sufficient reason was provided by a physician's analysis. Nevertheless, a mother desperate to protect her young son's life took it upon herself that day in insisting that Jason's condition be examined in the proper way. As she was adamant that the procedure be performed, the staff finally relented and prepared Jason to have the MRI.

A nurse took Jason back to an examination room, and Jason waited for a technician to administer the medical scan of his brain. Later, while examining Jason's brain via the MRI, a doctor halted the imaging process halfway through the scans, removed him from the imaging area, and rushed him into emergency surgery. Jason's mind began to race. He thought, *Am I going to die right here in this hospital?* Within minutes, succumbing to the anesthesia, Jason was unconscious while the doctors opened up his head and began to operate. After a few hours of surgery, Jason was placed in the recovery wing of the hospital. Before he came to, his mother and father awaited his return to consciousness with a great deal of anticipation. As Jason awoke, he was greeted by his parents. Then the surgeon entered to assess Jason's condition.

The surgeon asked a strange question that Jason will never forget: "Jason, do you remember how you got here?" The doctor gazed at Jason in amazement, as if he were looking at a ghost.

Jason was perplexed by such an odd question but responded with the pragmatism of any thirteen-year old mind: "My mom drove me, and then I followed the nurse down here." The doctor shook his head, doubting the legitimacy of his own professional diagnosis. "That's impossible. You had so much fluid in your brain that you should have been in a coma. You were very close to death, young man," stated the doctor with firm unrest.

One might question the doctor's lack of tactfulness in sharing the troubling news with Jason, but the doctor, himself, had stepped out of character for a moment, unable to conceal his own amazement. Jason was blown away upon hearing such horrible news—at first, he doubted its validity. After all, he was just thirteen years old. Thirteen-year-old kids are not supposed to think about death and sickliness. He had soccer games and baseball games to play, girls to chase, and brothers to harass. Suddenly, however, this thirteen-year-old boy, who had probably not thought deeply about life and death much before, began to think very deeply about his own mortality. Often when people are confronted with news about impending death, they begin to question the very meaning of their own lives—how much value it really has and if they have lived a productive life. At thirteen years old, Jason had not really lived long enough to successfully answer these harrowing questions, but yet he was forced to come to grips in this moment with the narrow void between life and death. Life and death are inextricably linked to each other. No living creature can feasibly have one without the other. In order to live, you must die; and likewise, if you have died, you most certainly were at one point alive. Of course, these kinds of thoughts were of no consequence to Jason just a week earlier, but when a doctor in a hospital tells a young man in a hospital that he is lucky to be alive, it is impossible not to sense the absolute fragility of life.

During the operation, the surgeon confirmed that Jason had an extreme case of hydrocephalus—a condition in which there is an excess buildup of cerebrospinal fluid in the ventricles of the brain. In Jason's case, a benign tumor barely the size of the tip of one's pinky finger was the cause of the blockage of the cerebral aqueduct in the brain stem. The emergency procedure performed by the doctors that day consisted of placing a shunt—a tubular device that would divert fluid away from the brain—inside Jason's head. This life-saving measure would serve as a man-made substitute for the cerebral aqueduct. Unfortunately, the surgeon determined that the tumor was inoperable since it was at the very bottom of the brain stem. While the sophisticated technology was available to divert fluid away from the cerebral aqueduct, removal of the tumor within his natural cerebral channel was considered far too risky for comfort. In the months that followed, Jason's family consulted four to five doctors all over the United States regarding removal of the tumor, and most of them, including Dr. Ben Carson—the world's greatest pediatric brain surgeon—determined that the surgery to remove the tumor was very dangerous and posed too great a threat to Jason's life. In sum, Jason had the best kind of tumor to have because it was benign, but it was in the worst place possible—at the bottom of his brain stem, which meant that it was essentially at the very center of his head. Most of the doctors agreed that the tumor would more than likely remain benign for the duration of Jason's life.

Now, Jason awoke to discover that the procedure had been successful, albeit with a throbbing headache and some disorientation. The doctors had rescued him from a potential catastrophe. Jason and his parents were relieved, hoping that now Jason could return to the normal, active life of a thirteen-year-old kid. However, Jason would have to learn to walk again and move around normally. Recovering from brain surgery oftentimes means that certain areas of the brain are temporarily affected, and in this case, some of Jason's basic motor skills needed to be rehabilitated.

The doctors explained, however, that the average shunt would be functional for only about seven years and that Jason could expect to have surgery again in due time to replace the temporary fix. Jason would more than likely be in his second or third year of college when the shunt would need to be replaced. He would need to have routine check-ups to determine how the shunt was holding up over time. If the shunt stopped working or broke, it wouldn't take long for the family to recognize it, as Jason would probably start to express noticeable discomfort, shaking, headaches, and lapses of memory.

Even so, as if Jason had not already experienced enough trauma, while he was recovering from the operation, he had a bad reaction to the anesthesia that caused him difficulty with urination. He went almost two days without being able to urinate. After Jason attempted to use the bathroom several times, he was catheterized. This reaction would have a drastic effect on Jason for the rest of his life as it had caused permanent damage to his bladder. Over the course of two days, his bladder became permanently enlarged. This suddenly resulted in a superhuman ability to drink a great deal of water before ever having to use the bathroom. While this may seem like an advantage, an oversized bladder meant that Jason was much more susceptible to bladder infections and could be faced with other potential health problems later in life.

Many people would perceive Jason as the type of kid with bad luck, but not Jason; he continually drew upon a positive outlook formed from a concrete foundation of faith in the Lord. Genesis 50:19–21 states, "Don't be afraid. Am I in the place of God? You intended to harm me, but God intended it for good to accomplish what is now being done, the saving of many lives." In this passage, Joseph is addressing his brothers who sold him into slavery in Egypt. Through resilience and faith in God, Joseph achieves unlikely success as Pharaoh's top advisor and becomes very wealthy and renowned. Similarly, Jason had been unfortunate. While this bad reaction to the anesthetics had permanently harmed him, the Lord had given Jason a distinct advantage that he would not fully appreciate until approximately seven years later.

Soon after the surgery, Jason went home sporting a fresh scar on the back of his head that mesmerized his four brothers. All of them had scraped up their knees and elbows or even broken bones, but it was hard to compare any of those injuries to the giant scar and stitching on the back of their brother's head. From a very early age, all of his brothers and his parents had noticed an inner toughness—a resilience—about Jason that just seemed to come naturally. He kept a positive attitude despite the situation, and the bright side always seemed to outshine even the grimmest of circumstances. While many kids would be down and out or even lethargic in such a state, Jason beamed with confidence and joy in spite of everything. Soon, he would be right back out there playing sports and doing all the things thirteen-year-old boys do. After all, he had seven years before his next surgery—half a lifetime for him. It would be a long time before he would have to worry about anything again.

Despite his positive outlook on things, the shunt that was installed inside Jason's brain lasted only six months. Within just a few months after the surgery, he began to experience the irritation of daily tremors and an increasing inability to concentrate or stay focused on a task. Now, the tremors in his hands were accompanied by extreme fatigue. Again, Jason was rushed into surgery, and the surgeons acted quickly to replace the shunt in his head. He awoke hours later to discover he had survived his second brain surgery in less than six months.

Over the next few months, Jay and Patty received all kinds of calls from neurologists suggesting that an operation be performed to remove the tumor. While many doctors agreed that the operation would be deadly or leave Jason permanently disabled, some were eager to perform surgery on Jason. At a loss for what to do, Van expressed to Patty and Jay that they should ask all the neurological surgeons suggesting brain surgery to produce five examples of successful outcomes that were similar to Jason's case. Jay and Patty agreed and submitted the request to the doctors. After the results were returned, Jay and Patty learned that most of the surgeries had left the respective patients permanently disabled, but on the other hand, some of the doctors warned that leaving the tumor inside the brain would eventually lead to death. Faced with a major dilemma, Jay and Patty decided that they would trust in God that the shunt would work effectively this time and hope that the tumor would remain in check.

When asked about this crucial moment in Jason's life and whether or not Jay and Patty made the right decision, Van shared this story: "I was in Portland for business, and I went to a happy hour at a sushi restaurant there. There were two empty seats at the bar, and one of the seats was next to a young lady who had a walker that could also be used as a chair. I thought, *I am going to sit there because I bet she has a good story.* The young woman had a hard time talking to me, almost as if she had a kind of cerebral palsy. I asked her about her condition, and she said that she ended up this way after the doctors removed a brain tumor from her brain. I am confident that if they had operated on Jason, he would have ended up the same way—permanently disabled. Jay and Patty definitely made the right decision for their son."

In a few short months, Jason's life and his physical body were forever changed. He was completely bald, had an underactive bladder, and was faced with possible brain surgery every seven years for the rest of his life. In addition, he now was sporting two noticeable scars on the back and side of his head, which stood guard over the shunt that protected his life. Jason, however, saw the scars on his head as bragging rights, so when asked by friends or strangers why he had them, he would playfully respond, "I was hit by lightning." When his questioners responded with doubtful replies or further inquiries, he would continue, "I was kidding. These scars are actually the sign of a great Native American warrior." Little did Jason know, of course, how appropriate his comment was, for just 150 years prior, Chief Okemos of the Chippewa tribe had boasted about a similar scar acquired during his battles with the American Cavalry.

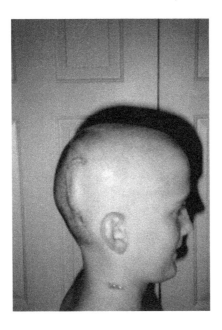

Jason after his first brain surgery, age thirteen.

To this day, doctors have never explained how Jason survived the surplus fluid on his brain. There are simply no satisfactory medical explanations for his physical resilience. There was something special about Jason James Merkle. He had more than physical toughness; he had supreme spiritual strength. If anyone were to ask Jason about this phase of his life, he would tell you, "The Lord was teaching me to trust in him and him alone."

Believe in miracles! Try to see the good in every situation. Have an eternal perspective.

9

Chapter 2

Alaska and Africa

I n Jason's own words, "Life seemed simple as I progressed onward through middle school and high school." The shunt inside Jason's head worked effectively and without any hiccups. Jason was grateful not to experience any major surgeries or emergencies for the next several years. When the first shunt broke, he and his parents had become very concerned that he would have to have surgery every six months for the rest of his life. That would be a tedious existence, indeed, as recovery from brain surgery is no walk in the park, even at such a young age.

In 1997, when Jason was sixteen years old, he was given the opportunity to go on a two-week trip to Glenn Allen, Alaska, and stay at Alaska Bible College. While in Alaska, he began to realize how fortunate he was despite his own trials. In many parts of Alaska, the average age of grandparents was only thirty-two years old. In addition, the land was riddled with alcoholics, the suicide rate was sky high, and the AIDS epidemic was on the rise. It was on this mission trip that Jason had his first adult confrontation with the Lord. There, in Alaska, far away from home and family, Jason felt the Lord calling him to go to the opposite end of the world to serve him—the sprawling continent of Africa. This calling from the Lord did not exactly please

Jason. From all the things he had seen on the *Discovery Channel* about the continent of Africa, the land appeared uncivilized, and the people looked like savages. The imagery in Jason's head consisted of people walking around buck naked with multiple piercings and war paint smeared on their bodies. All the same, Jason's heart had been pierced by the suffering he witnessed in Alaska, and when he prayed about what he could do to help, the Lord unexpectedly responded by calling him to go to Africa. Here he was in one of the coldest areas on the planet, and the Lord was calling him to leave and go to one of the hottest places. Truly, this must be from the Lord because Jason had no desire in his heart to go there. He did not feel prepared to comply with the Lord's request at this time. Jason's response was an ultimatum: "Lord, if you make this an awesome summer for me, I'll do it. I'll go to Africa."

For the rest of that summer (five weeks), he was an assistant coach for soccer camps throughout Michigan and Ohio led by an organization called On Goal, headed up by former Cedarville University star Tom Fite. On Goal is a Christian-centered soccer organization founded in 1985 that works to teach kids basic, fundamental soccer skills while at the same time increasing their knowledge and awareness of God's sovereignty in their lives. For Jason, this was one of the greatest summers of his life—he was healthy, active, and traveling away from home. Everything during this period in his life seemed easy. It was during this time that Jason nearly forgot about Africa altogether, and what's more, the days of his brain surgery seemed long behind him. Jason had resumed the excitement and joy of his youth.

As high school began to wind down, Jason started looking seriously into which school would become his university home. While he was intently interested in several universities, his parents highly encouraged him to attend Cedarville, which was a Christian university right smack in the middle of the heartland of America—Ohio. Jason, however, expressed no interest whatsoever in Cedarville. In fact, he tried to avoid the university at all costs. As he later admitted to himself, he somehow knew that if he attended Cedarville, he would undoubtedly be placed in a prime position to carry out God's

11

plan for him to go on an African mission trip. In a way, Jason started to wrestle with God during this season of his life. Despite his trials and his faith life, things seemed relatively good at the moment; he was active and vivacious enough now that personal health matters seemed to be light years away. Moreover, Jason was not thrilled with what God had revealed as a plan for him. In his heart, he had no desire to go to Africa, and in Jason's mind, if he could simply go to a public university like most other kids, he could avoid being inundated by God's call for him at a Christian university.

However, his parents persisted. They encouraged Jason to attend Cedarville for one semester, and if he did not like it, he could transfer to a different school. Jason reluctantly agreed. From that point on, there was no looking back. Jason fell in love with the people and the atmosphere at Cedarville University within about a week. Most of all, he enjoyed the Christian roots of the school, and for at least a time, the prospect of going on an African mission trip receded. He would focus on his major of organizational communications and move forward from there. In a way, Jason wanted a normal life—a life not consumed with an urging to go to foreign lands or perform duties outside his comfort zone.

As is the case with most college students, the first two years of Jason's tenure at Cedarville University were filled with a great deal of newness—new friends, new knowledge, and new adventures. Every day was different, and Jason and his good friend, Ben, spent a great deal of time doing the things that young, seemingly invincible young men do. For instance, there was a thirty-foot-tall waterfall in the area that Ben and Jason would jump off of each and every day, rain or shine. Sometimes the water was freezing, and the jump was always dangerous. Yet danger is a young man's greatest friend, for it is danger that encapsulates all the aspects of an epic journey for which a man's soul is designed. It's not a place or an object or even a concept that can be defined; it's just simply exhilarating and treacherous and worth conquering. Each day they would go there and make the leap, somehow avoiding harm. Jason testifies that his feet would hit the bottom of the small river below each and every time he jumped, yet he never cut himself or sprained an ankle. One could argue that he was exceptionally fortunate.

One day, as Jason and Ben were coming back from their jump, a few of the ladies from the women's cross-country team noticed that they were soaking wet and asked where they had been. They explained that they had been doing their daily ritual of plummeting into a thirty-foot ravine. The girls asked if they could meet them there the next day and give it a try. Jason and Ben looked at each other with smirks, wondering if these women had the guts to make the leap. "Sure," they replied. "We'll be there at three o'clock. See you then."

The next day, Jason and Ben were running just a few minutes late, and as they approached the waterfall, they noticed that the girls were being escorted by the police to their vehicles. The police had caught them jumping over the waterfall and decided to arrest them. Jason and Ben scurried to hide themselves from view, all the while chuckling at the girls' bad luck. After the girls and police disappeared from view, they performed their daily ritual, splashing into the water below. *Some people are lucky, and some are not*, Jason thought. While Jason and Ben felt terrible about the girls' misfortune, it did not stop them from returning each day to jump. They were never arrested by the police.

Following Jason's sophomore year, he decided not to return to be a coach for the On Goal summer camps. Each of the previous four years, he had coached young kids in soccer and ministered to them about the love and grace of Jesus Christ. This year, however, he would accept an opportunity to work at Michigan State University in the athletic department, working with John Lewandowski, which included baseball, football, basketball, soccer, and field hockey. While Jason was a diligent worker, he admitted that he began to feel abnormally fatigued during this time. Embarrassingly enough, Lewandowski discovered Jason sleeping on the job on more than one occasion, which was completely out of character for Jason. Something was not right, and Jason began to suspect that something was wrong with the shunt inside his head. Jason knew that God had uniquely placed him in this internship during this season of life, and yet he was having trouble committing to the entire workday. A feeling of dread began to creep over Jason as he wondered if he would have another brain surgery very soon. Persisting through the unexpected weariness, Jason worked as hard as he could performing his duties. He knew he had a doctor's appointment coming up soon enough, and perhaps God was forewarning him of a trial ahead.

Trust God. Listen and obey him, and he will direct your paths. Be willing to step outside of your comfort zone. The journey is always worth it.

Chapter 3

The Worst News

E ach year Jason had a check-up and an MRI with the doctor who had completed the shunt surgery in 1995. For seven years, his shunt had been operating effectively, and Jason had experienced no trouble. The year 2001 seemed as if it were smooth sailing too, except that Jason was feeling abnormally tired. He and his parents went in for his annual check-up in June. The technician performed the MRI, and the doctor called Jason the next morning. The doctor stated, "I need for you to come in tomorrow." Jason hung up the telephone not necessarily suspecting that anything was wrong but assuming that the doctor may be leaving for vacation and needed to meet with him beforehand. After all, it seemed doctors were always ready to go on vacation after seeing him. Jason Merkle was born an eternal optimist, and that would never change. Proverbs 16:3 states, "Commit to the Lord whatever you do, and your plans will succeed." This is the mentality with which Jason approached the results of his MRI. A fearlessness permeated his existence.

When Jason arrived at the doctor's office, the doctor asked Jason and his parents to have a seat and proceeded with the verbal results of the MRI. He said, "Jason, I have the worst news you are ever going to hear." A lump formed in Jason's throat, but he had heard awful news before, so he knew how to brace himself for a bad diagnosis. The doctor paused with a frown on his face that was impossible to hide. Jason tensed up in his chair as his mother and father squirmed to the edges of theirs. "Jason, the benign tumor in your brain has transformed. It is now malignant." His mother put her hand over her mouth as Jason looked around the room in search for answers.

Jason replied, "Does that mean it is cancerous?"

The doctor nodded with trepidation and continued. "Yes, it is a brain stem glioma, which is a rapidly growing tumor. I have called around to all the brain surgeons I know, and no doctor will even attempt to perform surgery. The position of the tumor is quite troubling, and any surgery to remove the tumor would probably be fatal. Essentially, the brain stem connects the brain to the spinal cord," the doctor explained. "It is located in the lower part of the brain (just above the back of the neck). The brain stem regulates breathing, heart rate, and the nerves and muscles used to see, hear, walk, talk, and eat."

His mother rose from her chair in a state of disbelief. "Well, what kind of treatment options do we have?"

"Chemotherapy and radiation are the suggested treatment options, but unfortunately, we have no record of any survivors of malignant brain cancer in the brain stem," the doctor replied. "We estimate that Jason has anywhere from two to twelve months to live. Over the course of the next few months, Jason's sight, hearing, and motor skills may begin to be affected."

Jason's mother gasped, as Jason remained speechless for several moments. Jason's father, Jay, was in shock as well. The room was quiet as they all looked at each other with a great deal of anxiety, fear, and sadness. Coming to grips with such a life-altering diagnosis takes several weeks, if not several months, for most people, but the Merkle family realized very quickly that they didn't have that long. Jason felt a great wave of sadness and fear pass over him, as he thought about the entire scope of his life. Currently, he was working in East Lansing for the Michigan State Spartans' athletic department as an intern, having the time of his life interviewing players and attending sporting events.

The next year would be his junior year in college, in which he would really begin to delve deeply into his major. Now, all of that seemed to be whisked away in one brutal diagnosis. How could this happen? If only it had been a possibility for the doctors to have removed the tumor when he was younger, this would not even be an issue now. Darkness and despair might have covered young Jason if it were not for a fervent belief in God. Romans 8:28 states, "And we know that in all things God works for the good of those who love him who have been called according to his purpose."

Jason's eternal optimism would not be repressed for long. "I don't know when, and I don't know how, but I am going to beat this," Jason stated affirmatively to both his doctor and his grieving parents. Jason's father nodded and smiled, quickly affirming Jason's confident assertion that he could beat even the grimmest of diagnoses.

The doctor smiled. "I hope you're right, son. In the meantime, I suggest you make a list of things you want to do and do them." This was a pragmatic response from a doctor who was staring face to face with medical reality. From a human perspective, this was unbeatable. Even with the recommended chemotherapy and radiation treatments, there were simply no survivors of brain cancer situated at the bottom of the brain stem. Since the tumor was inoperable, chemo and radiation may only extend Jason's life by a few months, albeit only prolonging the misery of a gradual decline in the midst of harsh side effects from the treatment.

Jason looked to his parents, who were aghast with the news that would shock any parent to the core of his or her being. The three of them clearly understood what the doctor was implying. There did not seem to be much hope, and given a formidable prognosis of only two to twelve months to live, they had better do all the things they ever wanted to do together in the next several months. Jason's time was very short, and things were likely to get bad very quickly. The three walked out of the doctor's office that day, and they knelt down together on the sidewalk leading from the doctor's office to the parking lot. They joined hands and prayed fervently to the Lord for wisdom, guidance, and healing for Jason. Despite such terrible news, their faith in the Lord Almighty was unwavering. God was sovereign, and God was good. The power of the Lord Jesus Christ to heal people from the worst diseases and afflictions is attested to through multiple accounts in the New Testament. Why should Jason be any different? There is always hope when we put our trust in the God of the Bible—and they all knew that God would never leave their side, even in the direst of human trials. Romans 5:3–5 states, "We rejoice in our sufferings, knowing that suffering produces endurance, and endurance produces character, and character produces hope, and hope does not put us to shame because God's love has been poured into our hearts through the Holy Spirit who has been given to us."

That night, Jason went in to work his last night at the local Pizza Hut. His good friend and coworker, Sarah, was the first person Jason told about the cancer. She was devastated to learn that he would not be returning to work with her anymore and that his life was in great jeopardy. They made smoothies and reminisced about their time working together. Jason admitted that he was going to have to drastically change his diet. There would be no more pizza, and this would probably be his last smoothie for some time.

Seven years back, Jason had been water-skiing, enjoying the carefree life of a young boy when his uncle Van noticed the tremors in his hands. A few days later, he was told he was lucky to be alive due to a blockage in his cerebral aqueduct. After surviving two brain surgeries as a young teenager, and now on the verge of adulthood, Jason was being told he more than likely had less than a year to live— the sinister cyst that had caused such a great deal of trauma already in its benign state was now working to inflict death in merciless fashion.

Imagine being told by a professional underwater scuba diver that most human beings cannot survive beyond two minutes under water without oxygen. "Some people," he says, "only can last about one minute and thirty seconds, with the world record being twenty-two minutes. You are going to be submerged in water for thirty-three hours. Essentially, you have no chance for survival." This is how bleak Jason's prognosis seemed.

Don't ever give up! With God, all things are possible. Stay positive and don't worry—it will only make things worse and never brings benefits.

Chapter 4

Burzynski and New Hope

Following the diagnosis, Jason and his family began to explore treatment options. They traveled to the University of Michigan to have a PET scan done of his brain to learn more about the tumor that Jason was fighting. It turned out that the PET scan involves a high-density glucose solution given intravenously in order for the scan to detect the cancer. Cancer is attracted to glucose, and this procedure actually caused Jason's tumor to begin to grow. By the time they got out of the hospital that day, Jason's eyelids were half closed as the tumor began to wreak havoc on his body. In fact, when Jason went to renew his driver's license just a couple of months later, he failed to see and name even the largest letter in the optics machine. He was considered legally blind.

After traveling to several medical centers and speaking with multiple hospitals nationwide, Jason and his family decided against traditional chemotherapy and radiation treatment. They sought advice from the following cancer centers: Johns Hopkins, Brigham and Women's, Henry Ford Brain Tumor Center, University of Michigan, and MD Anderson. While all of the oncologists at these centers recommended chemotherapy and radiation, all the experts proposed a different recipe for Jason's treatment. Some wanted to do more intense chemo and radiation over a short amount of time, while others suggested smaller doses over a period of time. All of the centers had one thing in common: they offered no long-term hope for survival. Some specialists even wanted to biopsy the tumor. When Jason's father asked about the side effects of the biopsy, most experts admitted that there was a strong chance that it could cause Jason multiple cognitive problems.

Jason's dad explained, "Everybody wanted to do the biopsy of the tumor, but it was not going to change how they treated the tumor. Their prescribed method of treatment was still chemotherapy and radiation. Thus, these centers wanted to do a biopsy for their own research purposes, and they were not primarily concerned about our son." He continued, "As we sat in the waiting rooms of these centers, we observed the patients—there was loss of hair and facial distortion, and this was not very comforting. When we asked to meet with any survivors of similar tumors, the doctors responded that that was a violation of medical privilege between patient and doctor. We finally came to the realization that these centers considered it a great success if the patients were still alive ninety days after chemotherapy or radiation treatment began. The patients usually die from pneumonia caused by the treatment." To Jason and his family, that sounded like simply trading one cause of death for another.

In essence, Jason's life and any chance at quality of life were written off by most of the doctors he visited. Jason's case was not only worth about two million dollars to the facilities, but moreover, he could prove to be invaluable to ongoing cancer research. Jason and his family recognized that there was absolutely no hope in going to any of these centers. None of these places had any record of survivors who had a condition similar to Jason's, except one: the Burzynski Clinic in Houston, Texas.

While the Burzynski Clinic's methods had been considered a US Food and Drug Administration (FDA) trial for many years, strangely enough, Burzynski had a record of cancer survivors, even those with tumors in the brain stem. The treatment was highly controversial in the medical community and, in fact, has been shunned to this day by highly regarded medical doctors as a problematic methodology for cancer treatment. Jason and his family, however, did not give much credence to the opinions of the medical community—Burzynski had survivors, and that meant hope. Facts were facts.

Jason and his dad even had an opportunity to meet and talk with survivors and other patients who were having success. It was a "no-brainer"—pun intended. The Merkle family would apply to the clinic to see if they would accept Jason for the FDA Phase II clinical trial. In this specialized trial, Jason would receive nontoxic antineoplaston treatment that had no permanent side effects. Jason was accepted to the program in late July 2001.

Dr. Burzynski's treatment is based on a revolutionary discovery of treating cancer patients with antineoplastons, which are chemical compounds found in urine and blood. They are composed of peptides and amino acids and are generally found to be depleted in patients with many kinds of cancer. Essentially, Burzynski's research was based on the theory that the body undergoes a process in developing new cells, and when these cells fail to come into fruition and a tumor develops, antineoplastons can transform an abnormal cell back into a healthy cell. Because Burzynski knew that peptides are natural carriers of instructions for cell development in the body, he began looking for the presence of peptides in the blood and urine of cancer patients. When comparing the blood and urine of healthy people to cancerous patients, Burzynski made a remarkable discovery: the levels of these peptides were decidedly lower in people with malignancies. The Burzynski Clinic first instituted its groundbreaking treatment in 1976 by infusing cancer patients with antineoplastons to help the body start producing healthy cells and hopefully eliminate tumors. Most significantly, antineoplastons are nontoxic. Unlike traditional chemotherapy and radiation, which attack both cancer cells and healthy cells, antineoplastons cause no harm to healthy cells. While it is still somewhat of a mystery how exactly the antineoplastons perform their eradication of cancer cells, it has been suggested that they serve as biochemical microswitches that shut down cancer-causing agents and activate the agents that fight cancer, most commonly referred to as tumor-suppressor genes. Regardless, many patients who have undergone treatment at the Burzynski Clinic have won their fights with cancer and gone on with their lives, with several testimonies available on the Burzynski website.

It was decided, then. Jason and his dad would leave to start the treatment at the beginning of August, while Jason's mother stayed with the younger boys, Jonathan and Jordan (the twins), to help prepare them for their college journeys. Jason's good friend from childhood, Ryan, a strong Christian himself, met up with Jason just three days prior to his departure to Texas. For three hours that evening, Jason and Ryan reminisced about their childhood adventures together as they "totally killed" Alan Jackson's song titled "Remember When," repeating the song over and over again for the duration of their discussion. It was during this time that Ryan spoke candidly with Jason about his diagnosis, not yet fully grasping the seriousness of his situation. Because of Jason's cheerful heart and inclination toward optimism, it may have been challenging for anyone to comprehend how dangerously near death he was at this point. Jason conveyed to him that the trials ahead of him were staggering, and this was important because it would not be long until Ryan's life changed drastically as well. One year later, Ryan would be riding his dirt bike on his mom and dad's farm when he would crash, breaking thirteen bones in his body. Not only was this devastatingly painful, but Ryan would come face to face with his own mortality just as Jason was processing it currently.

What's more, the following year, while Ryan and his buddy Nick were mowing lawns together (they owned a small lawn-mowing company and mowed lawns all summer), Ryan was chewing tobacco as they serviced a lawn in the neighborhood. Ryan hopped back in the truck for a moment to do some paperwork when he noticed a white, bubbly mass in his mouth. Ryan spit the tobacco out of his mouth, and immediately panic shot through his entire body as he contemplated having a malignancy like his good friend Jason. As Nick was putting the finishing touches on the lawn outside, Ryan sped off in his truck in a state of hysteria! Why had he chewed tobacco even after finding out about Jason's condition? How could he have cancer too? Ten minutes later, Ryan arrived at his house and ran upstairs to the bathroom to get a better look at the tumor in his mouth. He was sure it was cancer, without a doubt. His partner, Nick, was left holding the weed-whacker several blocks away, befuddled by Ryan's erratic behavior that had left him stranded in the neighbor's yard.

As Ryan poked around in his mouth, he was simultaneously bombarded by feelings of relief and embarrassment as out of his mouth popped the remains of a soggy, floury noodle. He had eaten spaghetti for lunch, and an unchewed part had been lodged in the back of his mouth! With embarrassment, Ryan sped back to pick up Nick, who was stupefied by the episode. For Ryan, a wake-up call on chewing tobacco had clearly been sent from above, which to this day causes Jason and Nick to roar with laughter.

The night before Jason left for Houston, several people from church visited the Merkle home to pray over him and his family, anointing Jason with oil as is the custom for such a vigil, calling upon God's swift healing. Hymns were sung that evening, and Jason still recalls the lyrics from one particular hymn echoing in his ears: "You are my strength when I am weak.... You are my all in all." What a privilege to have such a tightly knit church family who could be relied upon in the weakest of moments to lift one another up to the Lord, petitioning his intervention—an intercession, so to speak, of the Holy Spirit. "In the same way, the Spirit helps us in our weakness. We do not know what we ought to pray for, but the Spirit himself intercedes for us through wordless groans" (Rom. 8:26).

In late July 2001, Jason and his dad traveled to Houston to initiate the cancer treatment, trusting in the Lord to guide them through the arduous treatment process. The plan was to spend about three to four weeks in a hotel, commuting each day to the Burzynski Clinic before returning home to administer treatment. For many months from that day forward, not a day would go by that Jason and his family were not corresponding with the staff at the Burzynski Clinic.

The first night, they stayed at a hotel where there was a swimming pool. Jason had some energy that day and wanted to go for a swim. Jay thought it might not be a great idea, but he knew this might be Jason's last time to swim for a long while. With a port installed to administer medicine, swimming would not be an option. And if Jay was being honest with himself, he knew there was a possibility that Jason would never swim again. Finally, Jay agreed to let him go for a swim. Jason came back a little later completely exhausted—abnormally so for a twenty-year-old man. Jay recalls, "It was an Abraham and Isaac moment for me. I realized Jason was a gift. He is God's.... I am privileged to have him as a son. At that moment, I completely gave him over to God and trusted him to protect and care for my son. Ultimately, his life was not in my hands, but in the Lord's." In the twenty-second chapter of Genesis, God calls Abraham to offer up Isaac, his only son, as a sacrifice to prove his own faithfulness to the Lord. Just before Abraham performs the gut-wrenching deed, an angel from the Lord intervenes and provides a ram for the offering instead of Isaac. The Lord says, "By myself I have sworn, declares the Lord, because you have done this and have not withheld your son, your only son, I will surely bless you, and I will surely multiply your offspring as the stars of the heaven and as the sand that is on the seashore" (Gen. 22: 15–17). In essence, God tests Abraham's faithfulness, and Abraham passes the test. Likewise, Jay knew that he needed to put all of his faith in the Lord to care for Jason. After all, the God of the Bible is full of abundant love, grace, and faithfulness. He can be trusted, no matter how difficult things get and no matter what the outcome.

The next day, a huge blessing was hurled into Jason's path—one of the landlords of a nearby apartment complex generously offered for Jason and Jay to stay in one of his apartments free of charge. It turned out that this particular landlord had a son who had been miraculously cured of cancer through treatment at the Burzynski Clinic, and he decided that one way he could express his gratitude to the clinic for saving his son's life was to open an apartment up to out-of-town residents who needed a place to stay while being treated at the clinic. Jason and Jay were fortunate enough to be in the right place at the right time, and the cost savings for nearly four weeks was enormous. This was one of the early miracles during Jason's fight against cancer. Such generosity from a Burzynski benefactor offered hope and encouragement in these early days, when it was so important to stay positive and forward thinking—not to mention, they would need to save every penny they could in order to pay for the treatment process. The cost for treatment was a whopping sixteen thousand dollars per month since it was largely uncovered by insurance companies.

What's more, Jason's good friend Ben, a student at Cedarville University, came to visit him during his time in Houston. Ben had offered to do so in order to walk arm in arm with Jason as he went to the clinic each day and faced this gargantuan foe. The old adage that a person is lucky to find one true friend in this world is not accurate at all in the life of Jason Merkle—he had several friends, including Ben, who would rise to the occasion in big ways to support him in this epic battle with an inoperable brain tumor. While in Houston, they would spend time together in the evenings going to sporting events or simply sharing meals. In this way, Ben helped keep things feeling as normal as possible for Jason as he was grappling with a very abnormal reality.

During his time at the clinic, Jason met several other patients battling harrowing disease. There was Devon, who had come all the way from Canada. Devon started at the clinic on the same day as Jason, and the two of them spent the next three weeks at the clinic together before Devon returned home to administer treatment. Because Devon's tumor was not as precarious as Jason's, his tumor was no longer visible after two months of the antineoplaston treatment. Devon went off the treatment immediately after hearing the news, in spite of Burzynski's warnings that he needed to continue treatment for one year after the tumor disappeared. Devon and his family did not heed the warning, and his tumor returned. "There is a great temptation to celebrate before the finish," said Jason. "Just because the tumor is gone, it doesn't mean you're done." Jason and his family heeded this warning from Burzynski as they launched into his treatment.

Jason spent time with many others during his time in Houston. There was a lovely couple from Atlanta, Georgia, who had a four-year-old boy with a brain tumor. Another couple were there because both the husband and wife had cancer at the same time. Both were on the treatment simultaneously and encouraging each other through their battle. Their biggest fear, according to Jason, was not dying, but rather one living and the other dying. "There was comfort in the idea that they might die together or live on together," Jason said, "but they told me that if one died and the other lived, that would be too much to bear."

After almost four weeks at the clinic, Jason and his dad returned home to Michigan to begin the arduous task of administering six treatments over the course of each twenty-four-hour period. Every four hours, night and day, Jason intravenously administered the antineoplaston treatment—that is, for two and a half hours, Jason ingested the medicine via a surgically installed port, and then for the next one and a half hours, he rested. In essence, it took approximately two and a half hours for the medicine to be completely infused into his body, often leaving him exhausted. While the medicine was being infused, Jason walked around with the medicine pack (about the size of a fanny pack), which did not exclude him from all regular activity during that time. He was relieved to have an hour-and-a-half break at each interval to disconnect from the pump. By this time, however, the tumor had nearly doubled in size, and Jason's eyelids were beginning to shut. Moreover, he began to experience an indefinite ringing in his ears that made it difficult to hear or make voices out.

These were challenging days, as Jason was hooked up to the intravenous device twenty-four hours a day. Every twelve hours, the bags had to be changed, and every four hours, he had to pump a new regimen of antineoplastons into his system. In addition, he had to submit blood every other day and urine once a week to the clinic for lab work. To make matters more complicated, because the medical treatments that Jason received were high in sodium, Jason was abnormally thirsty all the time, and he will tell you that he drank three to four gallons of water a day (the average person at the clinic only drinks two). The Burzynski team told Jason that he would probably need to use the restroom about every half hour because of the amount of water he would need to consume.

However, God had shown favor on Jason long ago, and he did not know it. In 1994, when Jason had the first shunt installed in his head, his bladder had been irreparably enlarged, which at the time appeared to be a bad thing as Jason would always be more susceptible to infection and would not discharge urine at the normal rate of a growing teenager. Here and now, however, God revealed part of his plan for Jason in the form of blessing—Jason did not have the burden of having to use the bathroom every half hour, as his bladder was uniquely equipped to handle three to four gallons of water a day since it had been supersized by the faulty catheter just seven years earlier. Because Jason could drink larger amounts of water, he was able to flush his system more regularly, perhaps enhancing his chances of survival.

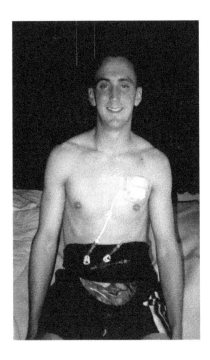

Jason with the port on his chest, ready for antineoplaston infusion.

Despite many blessings from God, Jason's life during this time was incredibly difficult. Every night, his parents would have to wake him up every ninety minutes to go to the bathroom. This was painstaking for Jason, as his body was so exhausted from the medical treatment, which caused severe drowsiness, not to mention the growth of cancer in his body, that it was inhumanly difficult to wake him up each night. On average, it took Jason's parents about fifteen minutes to wake him up each time at night. The consequences for not waking him up would be severe wetting of the bed.

Jason's dad elaborated on the grueling nature of life for the family at that time: "Those were long days. I had my own business, and I don't know how I would have managed life at home and the business if it were not for others stepping up for me at the office. God was so gracious to me to allow me to step away while others kept things going for me. The tumor continued to grow for a long time, and the family doctor was not going to support us anymore if the Burzynski treatment did not prove effective. Sometimes, Jason was so exhausted from both the cancer and the medication that he would fall asleep standing up."

One morning, Jason's parents went in to wake him up to use the bathroom, and Jason would not regain consciousness. Usually, it would take several minutes to wake him since his body was so fatigued. However, this morning was different—this time he was showing no signs of returning to consciousness. His dad began slapping him gently, pouring water on his face, and yelling at Jason with no success. Patty called the Burzynski Clinic, and they asked them to examine the dosage of medicine Jason was receiving. Normally, he was supposed to receive five hundred milliliters of the AS 2-1 variety and one hundred milliliters of A 10. However, on this occasion, whether by accident or by fluke, Jason had received five hundred milliliters of A 10 (the stronger blend) and only one hundred milliliters of AS 2-1 (the weaker solution). This meant that Jason's system had been rocked by the stronger blend of medicine. The clinic told Jason's family that he would probably sleep for two to three days and that they should let him do so. However, this was not a satisfactory response to Jason's parents. They spent the next two hours slapping, spraying, and yelling at Jason to wake up. They did not want him to be off his meds for that long of a period, and it seemed grotesquely unhealthy to allow their son to sleep for two to three days when the cancer continued to grow. Every day mattered in their minds—this was life or death each and every waking moment.

Finally, after two hours of slapping and spraying Jason a little more vigorously than what might seem normal, Jason woke up. In typical Merkle fashion, his parents yanked him out of bed and forced him outside to begin walking around the neighborhood. Jason remembers being intolerably exhausted, but his parents insisted that he had to stay awake and flush the overdosage out of his system as quickly as possible. This may seem like merciless behavior to some— Jason walked over four miles alongside his parents that morning—but the Merkles did not view their son's illness through traditional lenses. The way they saw it, sometimes the doctors did not give satisfactory answers to life-threatening problems, and they would often find their own way to combat the inertness (some would say lackadaisical approach) of the medical community's advice. In the beginning, it meant his mother's demanding an MRI despite the indolence of the CT scan doctor; at the onset of the cancer diagnosis, it meant choosing an alternative treatment that went against the advice of the family physician; and now, it meant waking their son up no matter how long it took to get his body working again as soon as possible so as not to waste precious time. Mistakes were mistakes, but the only way to effectively make up for a mistake was to remedy it with drastic action.

During the days, Patty was usually the caretaker. She was inexhaustible in her service to Jason during this time. Each day, they had to change the port bags regularly, draw blood for the clinic, and be sure that Jason was eating the right foods and drinking enough water. It is crucial, according to Jason, that someone who deeply cares about your well-being be there with you during times as trying as these. No person, without the assistance of someone else, could manage the day-to-day care that one needs, let alone remember all the little details. If she wasn't performing one of these duties, she was preparing food—especially hardboiled eggs, since he typically would not vomit after eating eggs. Jason's vomiting was caused by the effects of the steroid, Decadron, and his excessive intake of sodium.

On September 11, 2001, an unforgettable day, Jason was home with his mother. Jason was very sick when he heard his mom scream, "Oh my goodness! A plane just crashed into the twin towers!"

Jason recalls, "By the time I got into the bedroom, I watched the second plane crash into the second tower. I just remember that there was outright panic throughout the state of Michigan. It was difficult to get gasoline because people were filling up their cars. Churches were full all across the country. Our country went back to church and back to God after 9/11."

Truly, it is during times of crisis that people seek out God most fervently. It is only through the Lord that people excel to a state of incredible courage. Jason's battle with cancer was a microcosm of the larger evil wreaking havoc throughout the world. There are deadly forces at work all over in different parts of the world, be it disease, war, drugs, sexual perversion, or terror. The camaraderie exhibited by the people in the nation after 9/11 served as a metaphor for Jason—at the moment of devastating attacks, when all seems lost and there seems to be little hope, one can only overcome this kind of adversity through an active reliance on God's magnificent power to uphold the universe and all the tiny elements that are a part of it. Just when it looked like God had completely lost control, one had to remember that evil was not the result of the Lord's shortcomings, but rather mankind's. Disease and death are not the consequence of God's creative powers, but rather the nefarious result of original sin manifesting itself time and time again, generation after generation, as the world, in its brazen insolence, ignores and rejects God in an effort to create a new god it its own image. That god comes in many forms, but suffice it to say that freedom from the one, true God and his commandments ultimately means the dreaded dawn of hell on Earth. Ephesians 6:13 states, "Put on the full armor of God so that when the day of evil comes, you may be able to stand your ground." In sum, September 11 reminded Jason that he, too, was in a mighty battle against evil, and it was only a fierce faith in God that would bring him to the other side of glory, win or lose on Earth.

Search for success and follow it. Pray for miracles. Fight each day like it might be your last.

Chapter 5

Homecoming

On September 22, 2001, courtesy of his friends at Michigan State—most specifically, John Lewandowski—Jason and his family went to watch the Spartans play the Irish of Notre Dame in South Bend, Indiana. Lewandowski was a member of Jason's church, and he secured tickets for Jason not only to home games but also to highly desired away games such as this one at Notre Dame. The drive was only two and a half hours from Williamston to South Bend, but Jason was hoping to return home by the early evening for a special surprise. The Spartans won the game that day 17–10, and this ensured that both Jay and Jason would be in good spirits for the drive home.

On the way home, Jason told his dad that he wanted to surprise his cousin, Kylie, at the Williamston High School homecoming dance. Kylie adored Jason, and she was one of his greatest confidantes during his struggle with brain cancer. Kylie had been chosen as the homecoming queen, and Jason decided that he would show up unannounced (and three years removed from high school) to surprise his young cousin. He arrived about halfway through the dance and approached the DJ to make an announcement that a surprise guest desired to dance with the homecoming queen. The DJ agreed to do so, and upon making the announcement, Kylie's face vacillated among horror, embarrassment, and disingenuous glee—she thought maybe her ex-boyfriend had arrived to surprise her, and this would not exactly be a good surprise.

Jason revealed himself beyond the crowd of dancers, and Kylie's disposition immediately transformed from a state of ambiguity to one of absolute joy. Jason was decked out in a suit and tie for the occasion. Kylie scurried across the dance floor to greet him, and she and Jason danced together in a special moment for both parties. Kylie was indeed overjoyed that Jason had arrived to share her special moment with her. Kylie loved Jason so much that she even offered her blood in the event that Jason ever would need a blood transfusion.

Despite Jason's fervor, he was still feeling the negative effects of his tumor. Not only was the tumor growing, but the steroid he was taking puffed up his face like a balloon—he did not look like himself. Still, Jason was unabashed and unafraid to take center stage for the sake of his cousin's happiness. He knew this would be a welcome surprise.

Leaving that night, Jason delved into deep thought about his future. Here he was at the end of September, just over three months removed from his cancer diagnosis. While life had become much harder, he was still able to engage in regular activities such as football games and homecoming dances, all while the port in his chest ingested the antineoplaston medication. However, that would change very soon. Everyone knew that the tumor was growing at a speedy pace. Even if the medication was successful, the Burzynski Clinic had warned that the cancer would get worse before it got better. His treatment was an intensive process, one that resembled a marathon more than a one-hundred-meter dash. Jason thought about soccer too. He was down five to zero in the second half, and he had to find a way to come back and win.

Try to be a blessing to others. Make someone smile every day.

Chapter 6

Hallucinations

As the tumor grew, and it was growing quickly, Jason began to experience hallucinations. These were not just mild hallucinations—they were full-blown other-world experiences in which Jason would begin having full conversations with people who didn't exist. On one particular occasion, Jason was lying on the floor while his dad and his brother Matt sat upright on the couch. Jason would sometimes lie on the floor because he deemed it more comfortable. As he lay there, he began to see people and things all around him in a kind of super-altered reality. According to Jason, the hallucinations are hard to recall after experiencing them, but his new reality most definitely superseded the happenings of the real world. It's as if he had stepped into another dimension altogether and took on an entirely different self with entirely different people surrounding him.

As his father and brother looked on at this bizarre spectacle, it became rather frightening for them to behold a loved one beginning to lose his grip on the world around him. It certainly is not pleasant when Alzheimer's or dementia patients forget people and events right before the eyes of their loved ones, but this seemed worse as Jason seemed to check out completely, leaving behind a person who seemed to be sleepwalking while wide awake. Within a couple of minutes, Jason somehow broke the spell and came back to Earth, so to speak. Jay released the grip on his son's shoulder as he could see that Jason had broken the chains of hallucination, but he could not hide the dismay on his face as Jason gazed back upon him, finally able to respond normally.

On another occasion, Jason was at the mall with his family, and he told his mom and dad that he was going to venture to the sporting goods store to look around. They assented and told him they would meet up with him in a few minutes. While Jason was wandering around, again a new, unexpected reality gripped his consciousness, almost as if he stepped through the wardrobe doors in *The Lion, the Witch and the Wardrobe* (by C. S. Lewis). Jason awoke several minutes later as an attendant from the store asked politely if he needed help in some way, as Jason had planted himself cross-legged on the bottom shelf of one of the large racks. Luckily, his dad rounded the corner to find Jason not responding to the clerk. Jay lifted his son from the position and apologized to the store attendant, and Jason snapped back into coherence as they exited the store. "It was a scary time," said Jason. "We knew this could not be good that I was having hallucinations, as it most likely meant that the tumor was growing in full force."

In the medical community, hallucinations are grouped under the heading "Delirium." According to www.cancer.net,

> Delirium is a cognitive impairment disorder, meaning that it affects how a person thinks, remembers, and reasons. The main signs are sudden changes in consciousness or state of arousal, such as feeling drowsy or agitated. A person with delirium may experience confusion, disorientation, an inability to focus, memory problems, or changes in perception. These can include hallucinations or experiencing events that aren't really happening. Delirium is the most common sign of medical complications

of cancer or cancer treatment affecting the brain and mind. It is a common problem for people with advanced cancer or those at the end of life. Because of its troubling symptoms, delirium is often very stressful for the patient and family members.

This is spot-on what Jason experienced. These kinds of hallucinations often occur at the worst stages of cancer, often signifying that one is losing the battle with the tumor and may be nearing the end of one's life. This was certainly not lost on Jason's parents, but there was nothing beneficial about getting discouraged and thereby allowing this setback to defeat them. God could perform a miracle yet, and it was never too late for that.

In addition to the hallucinations, Jason began to experience a number of negative effects from the steroid, Decadron. Since the Burzynski Clinic treatments were considered an FDA trial, the FDA required Jason to take Decadron to coincide with his treatments. Supposedly, Decadron would work to decrease inflammation of the brain. According to Dr. Van Merkle, Decadron is an extremely dangerous drug that often results in kidney failure. Although Van discouraged Jason from taking the drug, both Jay and Patty felt they had to comply with the government regulations to avoid any kind of conflict in the Burzynski Clinic treatments. After a couple months of consuming the drug, Jason was experiencing several negative side effects, including insatiable appetite, external swelling, a ceaseless ringing in his ears, and the beginnings of kidney failure. In fact, when Van and his wife came to visit one weekend, Van noted that as soon as they arrived at the house that it reeked of urine, which indicated to him that Jason's kidneys were beginning to shut down. According to Van, during kidney failure, urine will sometimes begin to seep through the pores of patients' skin, causing a less-than-pleasant odor.

Jonathan, one of Jason's younger brothers, described this period in this way: "My most vivid memory happened during the fall of 2001. I was off at college and chose to go to school in Grand Rapids, Michigan, so I would be closer to home. There were so many unknowns at this point because Jason was recently given just months to live, and I felt in my heart that I needed to be close. I remember walking in and not even recognizing Jason. Before I could say hello, I had to excuse myself to the back room to collect what had just happened. I knew things were going to be bad but was not expecting to see such a physical transformation. The steroid Jason was on to help with swelling had, in fact, made his face swell almost unrecognizably. The swelling was so bad that he looked as if there was a deformity about him. I was so excited, scared, and sad, and my heart broke for a moment because I couldn't even fathom what he was going through. It was an eye opener, and I was preparing myself that someday soon I would have to say my final good-byes for his time on earth was very limited. No one can truly fully prepare themselves for what changes take place to our bodies during cancer treatment." The misery that Jason experienced was tantamount to that of a person slowly going blind and deaf simultaneously. His vision was poor, his hearing was failing, and he felt physically sick all the time.

Finally, Jason's uncle Van suggested to the family that they take him off the Decadron and begin trying natural anti-inflammatory substitutes such as Inflavanoid, which is essentially a ginger and turmeric compound. Van admitted, "I could never have suggested this to anyone but my brother or nephew as a nutritionist—specifically to go against a doctor's orders. I told Jay that the FDA can prescribe this to Jason, but he doesn't have to take it." With their backs against the wall, knowing that Jason's situation seemed to be worsening steadily, Jay and Patty agreed to try the Inflavanoid. Over the next several months, Jason's body began to respond well to these natural substances. God's grace was sufficient.

Keep your hope and faith no matter what the circumstances.

Chapter 7

Prankster

Jason Merkle not only possessed a cheerful heart; he was at heart a prankster refined and ready for any opportunity to render breathtaking laughs. Some people may regard his pranks as insensitive or even going way too far, but for Jason no such threshold exists.

On one occasion, after Jason had been taking steroids for some time, his entire body and especially his face were quite swollen. In fact, Jason did not look much like himself, as his eyes even seemed to be constricted behind his puffy cheeks, making it a challenge to see normally. Ryan Brannon, Jason's childhood friend, had seen him on several occasions in the fall of 2001, and it was obvious that Jason was not himself. For people who may not have seen Jason in a while, they might indeed be shocked by his appearance, as indeed his brother, Jonathan, admitted.

One day, Ryan and Nick were on their way to visit Jason, but Nick had not seen Jason for quite some time. Ryan warned Nick that he looked pretty bad and that he should prepare himself ahead of time. When Ryan went in to get Jason, Nick waited in the car. Jason explained to his friend that he wanted to have a little fun with Nick since it had been so long since they had come face to face.

Ryan agreed, and thus Jason's ploy was set in motion. Jason swung open the front door and stumbled out of the house, bent over in a kind of paraplegic state, with his arms swinging and dragging on the ground. His posture resembled that of a crippled orangutan, and the exaggerated arm swinging and stumbling must have been horrifying for Nick to witness. After all, who knew what a brain tumor could actually do to a person?

While Nick was frozen in a state of disbelief, Ryan could not contain his laughter. Falling over himself in painful fits of chuckling, Jason continued the charade until Nick finally went off on Ryan, yanking him from the ground and slamming him up against the truck, ready to pummel the life out of him. He was furious that Ryan was laughing at Jason's pathetic state. Ryan halted his laughter as Jason regained his normal posture and revealed his true state of being, pleading with Nick not to beat Ryan into submission.

Nick was infuriated, but Jason and Ryan erupted in uncontrollable laughter. Perhaps Jason had crossed the line, or perhaps this was exactly the laughter needed to sustain him, even if it was at Nick's expense. After all, to laugh at himself even in the condition that Jason was in helped him wrestle more effectively with all the depressing aspects of the disease. This prank was so successful that he pulled the same one on Matthew's wife when his brother and sister-in-law visited for Christmas that year. He acted it out so successfully that she fainted.

One other prank that Jason pulled happened around Christmastime, as he and his brothers Jonathan and Jordan decided to go shopping at the mall while they were home on winter break. As they arrived at the mall, Jason told them quite genuinely that he was not feeling up to going inside but would wait in the car for them while they completed the necessary shopping. It was December in Michigan, so his brothers kindly left the car running so he would stay warm. Of course, Jason would often get quite tired and could become unconscious, much like a narcoleptic. Moreover, the heat was blowing on his face, and who knew how long his brothers would be gone?

When his brothers returned just forty-five minutes later, as they were thoughtful brothers who didn't want their sick brother to have to wait in the car long, they found Jason passed out in the back seat. This was not good—it would often take fifteen to twenty minutes just to wake him up when his parents practically shook the life out of him as they sprayed water in his face in the middle of the night. And here his brothers were locked out in the cold with the car running! Both Jonathan and Jordan began pounding on the windows to try to wake Jason from his slumber, yet Jason did not budge. Onlookers going to their cars looked on with strange derision as Jordan and Jonathan pounded the windows of a car that was clearly fuming its exhaust out of the rear pipe. What's more, Jason wasn't visible to the people who passed as he was slumped over in exhausted stupor. Finally, after about two to three minutes, Jason popped up with a smile on his face, causing his brothers to fume well beyond what was coming out of the car's exhaust pipe. Jason unlocked the door roaring in laughter as his brothers scolded him with fury. Still, it was worth it to Jason in the end; he clearly knew that laughter was the best way to evade the allure of a lethargic state of mind and a discouraged heart.

As the young men drove home that day, it occurred to all of them that it did not seem right that Jason could eventually lose this battle with cancer.

A cheerful heart is good medicine. Smile and laugh a lot! Crying is okay too.

Chapter 8

Pastor Joe Dabrowski

In November 2001, Jason's conditioned worsened. He began to vomit quite regularly—he had a difficult time keeping meals down, and he would often throw up the vitamins his parents gave him. Often times, he was extremely fatigued.

Pastor Joe Dabrowski is one of the first people Jason speaks about in great detail when he describes his fight against cancer. At this time, Pastor Joe was the youth pastor at First Baptist Church of Okemos. Pastor Joe recalls the first time he met Jason in 1995:

> I can still remember the weekend I came to FBC to candidate in May of 1995. It was my responsibility to plan a youth night on Saturday at a local elementary school gymnasium, then on Sunday to teach the youth Sunday school class, amongst other responsibilities. We had a luncheon after the morning worship, and Jason was one of the teens who approached me and said, "I don't know what anyone else thinks, but I like you as our youth pastor." His words will forever be etched in my mind because that was the kind of kid Jason was. He was always positive in his attitude and

passionate with his actions. He was one of many teens who looked beyond themselves to impact and make a lasting impression in the lives of his friends. He was a key leader in our ministry and was always inviting his friends to come to our youth events. Our ministry would not have been what it was without Jason. Many Sunday nights we would find ourselves over at the Merkles' home with around twenty high schoolers who would gather together to hang out.

During Jason's illness, Pastor Joe was a continued source of support. On one occasion, he and John Lewandowski went to stay the night at the Merkle household while Jay was away on business. During the night, Jason had to be woken up to use the bathroom. Pastor Joe found out how incredibly difficult it was to wake Jason in the middle of the night. Pastor Joe said that sometimes it would take as long as five minutes to wake him, and when he finally woke, he needed to be helped to the bathroom, as he had a difficult time staying awake to urinate. Pastor Joe explains, "You would have to walk him into the bathroom and stand there with him—to ensure his safety. There was always the concern of Jason falling and his shunt closing. What a trouper he was. In perfect Jason fashion, he would be cracking jokes the whole time. Jason made it easy for those who sought to help him. Never did I ever hear him complain about his situation—not one time."

On one particular occasion, Pastor Joe and Jason decided to go golfing. It was good for Jason to try to stay active, even when he was not feeling 100 percent. Here's Pastor Joe's description of the day in his own words:

> Jason wanted to go golfing, and we had been planning a day when he would have enough strength. We were both terrible at the game, but it was good for him to get out, and I was willing to struggle through eighteen holes with him. He would pack his cooler

full of water and Gatorade, along with a snack for the afternoon. On this day it was hardboiled eggs. Jason offered me a bite after the ninth hole, and I graciously declined. The weather was warm. We had a great day of play and friendship. Jason needed to stay hydrated but couldn't seem to drink enough. By the time we finished eighteen holes and got to the car, he was weak and tired and not feeling well. I took him home and brought him in to the house. No sooner did he get into the kitchen did he begin to throw up in the sink. I have never seen anyone in my lifetime vomit so violently. It poured out of him—this is no understatement. This lasted for about a minute. Thereafter, he was feeling better and was back to his "normal self." That was Jason—never giving up and never giving in and never letting anything hold him back. Simply, as Jason struggled through his treatment, I, as well as others, wanted to be an encouragement to him. I don't know what Jason struggled with in his mind as he fought this disease. However, his attitude was beyond measure. It is each individual who determines their day through their attitude. We were there to help him through and believe that God could work a miracle in his life.

Simply put, Jason had a will to live. He was determined from the beginning to beat death even if it meant enduring a longer battle with cancer to do so. For many people, two to three months fighting this kind of sickness would have overcome them. Everyday living was hellacious. Most days were filled with exhaustion, violent vomiting, and four-hour intravenous antineoplaston treatments. Moreover, because of the amount of water that Jason was required to drink to keep his sodium levels at bay, he was using the bathroom between ten and fifteen times a day. The vomiting, on the other hand, was specifically a result of Jason's choice to quit taking the prescribed steroids cold turkey. As mentioned in a previous chapter, Jason had experienced a great deal of negative side effects from the steroids, including weight gain, enormous swelling, and kidney failure, not to mention difficulty hearing and seeing. When his uncle Van encouraged Jason to take the natural substance Inflavanoid to reduce the swelling in the brain rather than steroids, Jason switched immediately. However, users are supposed to wean themselves off of steroids over the course of six months, gradually reducing the milligram dosage each day. Because Jason quit cold turkey, he experienced intense vomiting for the next several months. Burzynski was nontraditional in his approach to cancer, and the Merkles fit right in, devising their own methods that were optimal for Jason along the way.

One day, when Jason was feeling well enough yet still not winning his battle against cancer, he approached Pastor Joe about writing a letter to all his friends and family who had offered support during his illness. He said, "I want to write a letter in case I don't make it. I want to be sure to thank everyone for all their support and prayers, and I want them to know that it has not been in vain."

Pastor Joe responded, "No, you should definitely not do that. God has bigger plans for you. If something does happen, I will write the letter for you." Over ten years later, Pastor Joe reflected on this comment to Jason.

> When Jason posed that question, he was well into his treatment. We didn't know if Jason was going to survive his tumor or not. Slow progress was being made; however, the future was very uncertain. I am a man and pastor who lives by faith despite the circumstances. Faith isn't asking God to show you the way and then you believe. You believe and then ask God to show you the way. As we prayed, we believed that God is and will ever be sovereign in all of his ways, and we petitioned God to heal Jason. We were living by faith and believing. I often thought of the centurion in Matthew 8:5–13 during this journey.

Rather than Jesus going to heal the centurion's servant, the centurion, who demonstrated a humble lifestyle said to Jesus, "Just say the word." We were asking Jesus simply to say the word and believing in God for a miracle.

One reason I told Jason to "keep the faith" is because that is what I witnessed through his life. In twenty years of ministry, I have walked beside many who have journeyed a similar path—a similar path which ends with a life on the other side of eternity. I've never known someone to handle such adversity like Jason. I was very close to Jason and was journeying this path with him each step of the way. Not only was he in our youth ministry; our family was close to their family. I can remember on a number of occasions our deacons gathering at the Merkles' house. We came together to pray over Jason. We believed God would heal Jason. We would meet in his family room, which was in the basement. We would surround Jason. And as he was seated and we were standing, we would lay hands on him and pray for him for forty-five minutes. Through many tears, we asked, even begged God to shower his grace upon the life of Jason. Jason was never a quitter, so to give up and have Jason write a note—that wasn't his personality and certainly wasn't how he lived his life.

Jason walked out of Pastor Joe's office that day having decided not to write the posthumous letter to his friends and family. His determination was renewed by Pastor Joe's strength and friendship. *Never plan your funeral*, he thought. *Always plan your future. The Lord does not intend for me to be afraid. He wants me to trust in him.* Jason would not be deterred, nor would he allow cancer to overcome his will to survive—no matter how bad it got. Jason never told anyone else about his desire to write the letter. Pastor Joe was his confidante and ally.

It was about this same time that the family physician approached the Merkles inquiring about the success of the treatment at the Burzynski Clinic. The treatment was nontraditional, to say the least, and everyone in the medical community, including the family physician, recommended chemotherapy and radiation for Jason's condition. Honest people that they were, the Merkles told their doctor that the tumor continued to grow but that the Burzynski Clinic indicated that this was to be expected since usually the cancerous mass would swell before it ultimately met its demise. With the antineoplaston infusions, one would often watch as the malignancy would actually seem to get worse before it got better. However, the family physician wasn't buying it. He said that for Jason to have any chance at all, he would need to switch to traditional treatments immediately, and despite the likelihood of success being very small in the long run, it was the only hope to extend Jason's life for a while longer.

The Merkles politely declined, demonstrating the patience required to not just trust the Burzynski Clinic's prognosis but believing wholeheartedly that God had led them to this alternative treatment. Besides, they were looking not just to extend Jason's life by a few months but to prolong it indefinitely.

As November drew to a close, Jason prayed that "Jesus would kick Satan," his father recalls.

Surround yourself with the right people. Have positive and good role models. Plan your future. Never plan your funeral.

Chapter 9

John Lewandowski
and Spinach Shakes

Among the people Jason expresses the most gratitude toward in his battle with cancer is John Lewandowski, assistant athletic director and director of public relations at Michigan State University. Lewandowski was a member of Jason's church, First Baptist Church of Okemos. In the months leading into the summer of 2001, Lewandowski helped secure an internship for Jason with media relations in the athletic department at Michigan State University. That summer (just prior to the tumor diagnosis), Jason had a wonderful opportunity to work and learn the ins and outs of running and maintaining a top-notch athletic department. Specifically, Jason was tasked with the duty of interviewing players in all different sports, including baseball, basketball, football, and field hockey. The information that Jason collected was incorporated into the media guide distributed to media personnel during home games. Jason was also present for many MSU golf outings, assisting where necessary and learning the particulars of all that went into putting on successful events for both home and visiting players.

For Jason, the MSU internship was a lasting memory that bled into and over the top of the cancer diagnosis. Lewandowski was kind enough to allow Jason to stay on board and work intermittently with the athletic department even when doctors' appointments and pressing obligations interfered later that summer.

The following fall, as Jason was in the midst of the worst of times in his battle for his life, Lewandowski stepped up big time and lavished football tickets to all Michigan State home games for both he and his friends. Every game, Jason was there, and not just in regular seats—in the press box! Lewandowski's generosity during this time cannot be overstated, as it gave Jason something to look forward to each and every week. No matter how bad he was feeling, and often times he was feeling awful, his buddies Matt, Ben, and John would join him for the games.

Before each game, Jason would force his three friends to drink a new dietary staple in his life during cancer treatment—the spinach shake. These shakes were not for the faint of heart, though they were high in nutritional value and ideal for someone like Jason, who had been taking intentional steps to assist his body in combating its malignancy. To show camaraderie, Matt, Ben, and John would drink the shakes with Jason, even if their stomachs churned as they did so.

One day before a game, Jason was feeling somewhat queasy but, for tradition's sake, downed the spinach shake before the game. After all, what was green and went down easily was always a good omen for the Michigan State Spartans, who donned the colors of green and white. This day, however, it didn't go down easily. Jason vomited the shake onto the kitchen floor and retreated briefly to the couch in the adjacent room to gain his composure. Ben and John comforted him as best they could and asked what he needed. Meanwhile, Matt had missed the spectacle as he was out of the room using the bathroom.

Just as Jason was getting up to clean up the mess he had made, Matt walked out and laid eyes on the kitchen floor. Kindly, Matt offered to clean it up, believing that Jason had simply spilled his shake. Jason insisted that it wasn't necessary and began to clean up his mess. However, Matt, trying to be a sympathetic and compassionate friend, told Jason to rest on the couch, saying that he had this and it was no big deal. Jason reluctantly agreed, as Ben and John both looked on in disbelief. Would Matt really scrub Jason's puke off the floor? Was he a saint and they didn't know it? What Matt didn't know was that Jason had puked at all—he simply thought he was cleaning up spilled spinach shake, not the partially digested form of the same. Halfway through scrubbing and cleaning it up, Jason noticed that Matt was not being particularly careful in cleaning up the mess and had much of the liquid all over his arms.

"Matt, thanks for cleaning up my puke," Jason stated.

"What?" Matt answered in disbelief. "That's disgusting! I thought this was just your spinach shake!"

John, Ben, and Jason burst out into laughter, expressing delight in their friend's generous misfortune. "Yes, that's why I told you I would clean it up," replied Jason. Needless to say, Matt was furious and began frantically washing off his arms in the kitchen sink. It was a moment for the ages—green shakes, green jerseys, and now a red-hot friend decked out in green puke for the Michigan State football game!

Let others be a blessing to you. This can be hard, but it's important. Eat as nutritiously as possible. Load up on greens!

Ben, Jason and Matt outside of Spartan Stadium.

Chapter 10

Death Draws Near

On November 18, 2001, the *Williamston Enterprise*, a local newspaper, published an article on Jason and his plight with brain cancer. The article began, "Jason Merkle is a humble man with a mission. He is out to prove that miracles exist." Of course, many miracles have happened throughout history. Simply put, miracles are unexplainable events or occurrences that cannot be reasoned through by scientific principles. The occurrence of miracles suggests that there is, indeed, evidence of the supernatural realm— that God exists and is active in the lives of humankind. Not long after this article was written, it seemed that a miracle was becoming more and more unlikely for Jason.

In early December, nearly four months into his treatment, Jason's parents rushed him to the hospital with a body temperature as high as 105 degrees. His eyes were almost completely shut, and he was having an incredibly difficult time hearing. At the hospital, the doctors confirmed that he had a severe staph infection. Morbid thoughts were racing through his mind as he lay again in the hospital contemplating whether this would be the last time he would ever go to sleep. In Jason's own words, "It was terrible. I kept thinking, *I can't die here. I have all those people I need to thank for how they have encouraged me during this time. So many people have prayed for my recovery, and I want to tell them how much it meant to me."* Jason's tumor had grown from fingernail size in June 2001 to the size of a golf ball—the prognosis was anything but encouraging.

To make matters worse, the doctors and nurses at the hospital had no luck in reducing the effects of the staph infection. They were pumping him full of antibiotics in an effort to eliminate the infection. Jason's situation looked dire, indeed. After ten days of battling high temperatures and loss of vision and much of his hearing, Jason's condition only worsened. His liver was failing, and his body was beginning to shut down for good. At this time, Jason can faintly recall hearing his mother sobbing as he drifted in and out of consciousness. In spite of his pitiful state, Jason kept thinking, *I can't die right here. Not now.*

On December 2, Jason's dad recorded this: "Praise God. Jason's hemoglobin is very low. His fever is not spiking quite so high. Ate three full meals and walked the halls. The family doctor would like a blood transfusion because of the hemoglobin. Please give us wisdom, Lord. Van said not to do a transfusion. Try and build blood back up with B12, trace minerals, and multivitamins." Here, Jason's dad is referring to Van, his brother, suggesting that they not do the blood transfusion. Blood transfusions carry enormous risks—Jason could have rejected the blood given to him and ultimately die, and there was always the risk of undetected disease transmission. Blood transfusions are safer today than they have ever been, but at the turn of the century, there remained a stigma about transfusions as related to possible transmission of HIV, along with other deadly diseases.

The next day, the Merkles' prayers were answered—Jason's hemoglobin levels miraculously increased, meaning that he would not need the blood transfusion after all. No one could reason why Jason's hemoglobin had suddenly risen, other than to credit it to God answering desperate prayers.

The bad news was that the staph infection was not getting any better. The antibiotics were simply not effective against it. Moreover, Jason's mother and father were extremely wary of the hospital staff's recommendations to use glucose-rich antibiotics. Because they are educated, they know that cancer cells grow with an increase in sugar in the body. For this reason, they requested antibiotics that were devoid of all glucose. Jay explains, "Patty or I were always in the room watching what was being put into our son's body. We were scared to death because the hospital staff did not know what to do."

Again, Jason's uncle Van, like an angel called onto the scene, made a suggestion that seemed absurd to the medical community around Jason: "Let's try some garlic oil and oil of oregano." Despite the strangeness of this suggestion, Jason's parents were desperate for options. Uncle Van had risen to the occasion twice before in Jason's life, so perhaps he was an answer to prayer this time as well. So they tried it, continuing to pray fervently that Jason would survive this onslaught of infection paired with the rapid permeation of cancerous cells.

On December 7, 2001, Jason's father recorded some excellent news: "We finally have a negative blood culture. We started the oil of oregano and garlic oil tabs on Thursday—there have been no antibiotic changes since Wednesday—therefore, the only change that may have made a difference is the oils." In essence, despite all the doctors' repudiations, it certainly appeared that the garlic oil and oregano oil were largely responsible for eliminating the staph infection. The high-powered antibiotics were no match for Jason's infection, but the natural herbs offered up by the Lord proved to be devastatingly potent against it. Much to the surprise of everyone, including the hospital doctors and staff, the next morning the infection was completely gone.

In short, something that was nothing short of miraculous had occurred. Jason had been knocking on death's door just twelve hours earlier, and now after consuming some of God's natural herbs, he recovered. In Jason's own words, "It was the first time we had a real sign of hope from God. I thought, *Man, God's got a plan for me.*" He added, "I saw a light at the end of this tunnel I was going through." Needless to say, the doctors and hospital staff were flabbergasted. His recovery was more than unlikely; it was impossible from a medical standpoint. However, the Lord Almighty is not limited by medical science, and for Jason and his family, this was yet another indication that the Lord would work uniquely in Jason's life story to glorify his name. It was a powerful moment for Jason and his family as they arrived home with a living, breathing, twenty-year-old man poised to continue his fight against death—that formidable, lurking, and irreversible truth that hangs over all humanity like the closing curtain to an insatiable stage performance.

Uncle Van has a unique perspective on the success of the herbs: "It's not widely known that natural herbs work. Doctors are employees, and they are medically trained. I mean, doctors have to generate income, and if you show cancer researchers or developers of antibiotics these kinds of results, they don't want to hear anything about it. Cancer diagnosis means about one and half million dollars in medical revenue for each diagnosis. It's not that these doctors are bad guys, but they don't want to know what else is out there because they have a livelihood."

After the Merkles arrived back home, it occurred to Jason's parents that the staph infection may have been caused by a malfunction in Jason's pump just days earlier as he was shopping with his grandmother. While in the store, his IV bag and fanny pack filled with blood because the antisiphon valve had not been installed correctly where it connected to his port. Therefore, the blood started clotting in his port, and the medicine was not being administered correctly. This oversight may have led to an infection getting into his bloodstream. It would be important to monitor the port and IV bags carefully going forward.

Soon after Jason arrived home from the hospital, he and his family all prayed together. They thanked God for rescuing Jason from danger and most importantly for healing. That night, Jason's brother Matt prayed that Jason would be completely healed in one year, which, incidentally, would be in December 2002.

Thank people for helping you. Don't be afraid to think outside the box.

Chapter 11

A Young Man's Beach

While Jason was still in the hospital battling the staph infection, he complained of left shoulder pain. Jay promptly checked it and discovered the area around his shoulder was severely inflamed and swollen. As he applied pressure to the area, he discovered that the pressure was mainly in Jason's chest. As Jay looked closely, he noticed that the skin around the port was blistered and began seeping pus as pressure was applied. After consulting with the doctors, Jason and his family agreed that the port would be removed, which meant he would receive no medicine while his skin healed—it seemed like another great setback was in the making. The doctors believed that this rash and infection were all symptoms of a lingering staph infection. Three days passed, and despite their efforts to have the port removed, which required a surgical procedure, it seemed to continually get delayed due to doctors' schedules or circumstances. On December 13, 2001, as the doctors were getting ready to remove the port, another small miracle occurred—the rash dissipated and the pus disappeared. "Praise God. The line can stay," Jay responded.

Following Jason's arrival home from the hospital with his staph infection effectively gone, Jason started to feel a little bit better. It seemed like the antineoplastons were starting to work. The family continued to pray fervently together each and every day.

During the daytime, his parents would turn on the Cedarville chapel service so Jason could hear the pastor and students praying for him. This was a great encouragement to him, as it was often difficult to think about missing out on his junior year of college. Jason, indeed, had many people praying for him at this time. Three to four friends and family members would visit him each week to offer encouragement, and he received hundreds of letters and care packages during this time from fellow Christian believers and acquaintances. In Jason's mind, he was never without hope because he had an army of prayer warriors appealing to God for a miracle in his life. Miracles happen to those who believe miracles are possible— who, in essence, put their faith in God and believe that, with God, all things are possible. To illustrate this, one of Jason's classmates at Cedarville made a small puzzle and shipped it to Jason inside a large envelope. When Jason constructed the puzzle, it read, "Be gracious to me, God, be gracious to me, for my soul takes refuge in you; and in the shadow of your wings, I will take refuge" (Ps. 57:2).

Each day, Jason's parents would insist that Jason ride his bike or walk at eight o'clock in the morning. He would ride or walk around the block to get some much-needed exercise, despite how bad he might be feeling. This was an effort to keep him moving and active, lifting his spirits even if only for a short time. Often, he would be exhausted afterward, but he was always in a better state of mind mentally, which was vital to his continued survival.

Of course, for the entire month of December, Jason had to be taken off of antineoplaston treatment because his system had been overloaded by antibiotics, and his blood counts were dangerously low. Strangely enough, at the end of this month, Jason had another MRI, and for the first time the results showed no growth in the tumor despite not being on antineoplastons. Hope was on the horizon in a tangible way now for the Merkle family—it was like seeing the sun burst above the horizon for the first time after months and months of stifling fog.

On January 7, 2002, Jason's dad recorded in his journal (which he wrote in nearly every day during Jason's illness) that Jason started to show signs of improvement. In reading his notes, one can read between the lines that Jason's father was proud of how hard Jason was fighting this deadly disease: "Jason is now at 160 lbs—great appetite. Rash is subsiding. He is quite tired and did 175 pushups tonight during the commercials of the Vikings/Raiders Monday night football game. He appears more awake and alert since being off steroids and antibiotics."

Just a few days later, Jay wrote, "Jason had many compliments on how well he looked at church today. He is feeling well. Praise God."

On January 16, 2002, he wrote, "Jason attended the MSU game tonight with Ryan. MSU won against Purdue! Jason stayed awake and alert the whole game! He is still getting up at night all by himself—praise God for his alertness!"

But on January 18, 2002, Jay reported some bad news: "Jason had the MRI yesterday. We were very disappointed to see growth. 2.6 cm x 2.5 cm x 4.7 cm. I spoke with the pastor, and we must pray on."

There had been numerous setbacks in Jason's fight against cancer. Almost as soon as Jason started feeling good and responding well to the treatment, they would receive some bad news or Jason would take a turn for the worse. Growth of the tumor was the worst news that they could hear because it appeared that Jason was losing the battle in spite of all the prayer and antineoplaston treatment. One month earlier, Jason had barely survived a staph infection, and now, it appeared that the tumor was thriving inside of Jason's head. Perhaps it would not be long now and any hope for survival would be lost altogether. Jason's prayer just a couple months prior for God to "kick Satan" seemed to be going unanswered—the small moments of triumph were being crushed by incessant defeats.

Dr. Ben Carson, the gifted brain surgeon, who had concurred with other surgeons that Jason's tumor was inoperable, says this in his book titled *Think Big*:

> When we develop a relationship with God and believe that He is working through us, we still have moments of helplessness—when God has an opportunity to do something for us. That happens when we give our best—which, at that particular moment, does not seem good enough. Ready to give up, we say aloud or silently, "I cannot do any more, Lord. I need You." At such moments we provide God with the opportunity to respond. Truly, "Man's extremity is God's opportunity." (251)

Jason and his family were at a breaking point. For nearly six months, they had endured the torture of endless medical treatments, vomiting, fevers, and numerous setbacks, including the staph infection and the continued growth of the tumor. But they had a supernatural weapon that kept all of them pushing on in spite of the maddening adversity—faith in God to deliver them to the promised land in spite of all the naysayers and all the discouragement.

One week later, Jason and his family traveled to Florida to escape some of the struggles at home. Perhaps some time away would be good for Jason, and it was hard to say whether this would be the last time he ever saw the ocean. Despite his trials, he stayed active, and he soaked in the beauty of God's creation. The immense body of water symbolized something for Jason as he walked upon the sands gazing outward—the ocean symbolized hope for eternal life in its broad, endless portion stretched out against the edges of the horizon.

On January 26, 2002, Jay wrote, "Jason ran at the beach—he seemed better after he ran and exercised. Jason is still not feeling as well as he did before, but seems to be improving a little each day. God is so good, as we pray each night for healing."

Two days later, he continued,

> Because of high sodium levels in his blood, Jason was no longer allowed to go out into the sea, and he had to walk with tennis shoes on the sand. Jason was

so disappointed but at least we now understand the source of his imbalance. He had just not felt good and was actually feeling worse since we had arrived here last Thursday. We removed him from the pump at 6 p.m. Dinner did not stay down (white fish). We got back to the motel and downed two raw eggs. (He has always been able to keep raw eggs down no matter how sick he has been). The eggs provide a source of protein and are easily assimilated. We took vitamins and minerals and a couple more raw eggs. Jason said it will be great to sleep for four hours straight without going to the bathroom every hour.

Without question, twenty-year-old men crave activity and adventure. It is at this point in life that a young man really begins to enter his prime—where his athleticism peaks and his sense of adventure is inundated with a curiosity and desire to explore. It's hard to adequately describe this time in a man's life, but John Eldredge comes as close as any in this explication from *Wild at Heart*: "Adventure, with all its requisite danger and wildness, is a deeply spiritual longing written into the soul of man. The masculine heart needs a place where nothing is prefabricated, modular, nonfat, zip lock, franchised, on-line, microwaveable." In this short passage, Eldredge comments on all men's inherent longing for precarious roads and destinations—for the unexpected and treacherous cliffs that present a worthy challenge. For if a man cannot build a bridge or swing across to the other side of the ravine, he cannot experience the satisfaction of achievement that God himself probably felt upon creating the world, which embodies such mysteries. Simply put, men (and especially men in their twenties) are as unruly in their impulses and urges as God intends them to be.

Jason still had these desires, but the prime of his life was being stolen away by a crushing disease. Just being able to run at the beach seemed thrilling to Jason's young body, but even this was now causing him harm. It seemed nearly everything was off limits for him during this time, and the frustration must have been equal to not being able to find water or food on a deserted island. There were times when Jason felt alone on this journey—even while so many people were praying for him and helping him along the way, he was, after all, the only one who was really sick. He was the one vomiting profusely, ingesting sodium-rich medication every four hours, and feeling perpetually debilitated while at the same time not being able to sleep for more than a couple of hours at a time due to his need to constantly use the bathroom. Imagine the worst sickness you have ever experienced, and remember how tired you felt and your need for sleep. Then imagine not being able to sleep without being woken up every two hours.

While at the beach, Jason's sodium levels in his body drastically increased—this was dangerous because high sodium levels could render hospitalization or even death. This was a dubious discovery for the Merkles because Jason's diet had not been sodium rich at all. They continually monitored what Jason ingested, and only on rare occasions did he treat himself to high-sodium foods such as pizza, soft pretzels, and French fries. It was later discovered that Jason's time at the beach had been the primary reason for his unusually high sodium levels. His body was absorbing the sea salt through his skin, and this would cause increased vomiting and diarrhea, making antineoplaston treatment impossible and useless.

Because of the elevated levels of salt in his body, Jason took a break from the antineoplaston treatment. While the water he consumed on a daily basis counterbalanced the high sodium present in the antineoplaston treatment, he could not possibly drink enough water to counterbalance the absorption of salt particles from the ocean through his skin and the treatment. So he got some much-needed rest for the first time in a long while. Perhaps the salt water from the Lord's ocean was meant as a blessing—to take a break from the treatment and rest in the Lord, knowing full well that it was God who was in complete control.

On February 2, 2002, Jason's dad recorded this: "We had a nice day at the Flea Market. Jason bought a blow dart tube and darts. Jason (using his marketing education) spoke to the bathroom attendant and encouraged him to smile and be friendlier, and that would generate more tips. Jason also spoke to a vendor selling hot sauce. This vendor had samples but was sitting down and showing little interest. Jason encouraged him to stand up and be friendly with people and offer them a sample. The man asked why Jason gave him the advice. Jason shared that he had taken some marketing classes and thought the gentleman should at least give it a try. The man thanked Jason and told him it was just the advice he needed."

Jay Merkle, Patty Merkle, and Jason, 2001.

This was the kind of disposition that Jason always carried, even during his illness. Despite not feeling well and battling the prospect of death each and every day, Jason viewed life through an optimistic and energetic lens. There simply was not enough time to live life in a depressed, downtrodden, or indolent state of mind. Jason's day-to-day life within the throes of cancer served as a testament to all those around him that there just was never an excuse for wasting a day given to them by the Lord. *If God wakes you up each day,* Jason thought, *then each waking minute should be spent in glorifying the Lord with your life.* To do anything less, according to Jason, was wasting the precious time that God had given to each person. He knew something more about the preciousness of time now—the Lord was using Jason's experience to communicate to others that the short storybook of one's life was predictably unpredictable, even volatile at times, but what mattered most was how one reacted to the tribulations of one's life. At its conclusion, whenever that may be, each life would be viewed by others and by God on how one responded to difficulties—for who was ever remembered for how they did the easy things easily? Rather, the heroes throughout history have been remembered for how they were never overcome by the hard things but instead welcomed hardship as an opportunity to excel and overcome. Simply put, Jason was the kind of person who made the hard things seem easy and the harder things seem even easier.

In February 2002, while still in Florida, Jason's dad recorded this: "Jason threw up last night and had little rest. He also threw up in the morning. Gagged on one of the pills. We went to church at 9:15 a.m. and after church went out for breakfast. Jason was very tired and weak. He slept all day. He was hooked back up at 2:00 p.m. We watched the Super Bowl together, and he ate quite a bit. He felt much better. He slept well all night just getting up as needed. We thanked the Lord as a family for another day!"

As the Merkle family drove back from Clearwater Beach, Florida, they decided to stop on the way home at Cedarville University so that Jason could say hello to friends he had not seen in a long while. It just so happened that the day he arrived was February 19, 2002—the day he turned twenty-one years of age. Twenty-five hundred people were gathered in the chapel that day when Jason arrived, and he was invited on stage by Pastor Rohm so that the entire congregation could pray over him. Jason gave an update on his condition, and just as he began to exit the stage, Pastor Rohm stopped him and had everyone in the congregation rise and sing "Happy Birthday" to him. Jason was delighted. While most men and women celebrate their twenty-first birthdays partying in a carefree state of mind, Jason was at war with a ferocious foe. In this moment of solidarity with Jason, as he marveled at how different his life was from those in the audience, he actually felt privileged that God had marked his life for a different path in spite of how much harder it seemed. Jason already had a maturity about him that would seem precocious to anyone observing a population of twenty-one-year-old men. He had realized much earlier than most that he was not invincible—that life was both given and taken away by the Lord Almighty, who had simply gifted us with a short time on earth. As he walked off that stage, he smiled and thanked God for fellow Christians to rely on during challenging times. And for the first time in a long time, he felt special in a good way.

After the service, one of Jason's close friends, Christi, greeted him. Jason clearly did not look like himself—he had lost a lot of weight and suffered a great deal in the previous months. After visiting with Jason for a minute, she called to warn a mutual friend of theirs, Mandi, that Jason did not look very good and that she should prepare herself for meeting him in a couple of weeks for lunch. Out of fear or shame, Mandi canceled her lunch with Jason later that week, not knowing whether she had the strength to see him in that condition.

It was only several weeks later that Mandi called Jason again and apologized to him, explaining that she had experienced some irrational fears about seeing him in such a state. People are likely to have all kinds of different reactions to seeing someone on the brink of death—for some, it's much too scary to witness because it reminds them of their own mortality and the grotesque aspects of human existence.

When human bodies are not healthy, it can get rather ugly. So many people take for granted being healthy and having all of their internal organs functioning in perfect synchronization with one another. However, perfect health is actually the exception to the rule rather than the rule, as much as people would like to view it differently. The Lord has constructed human bodies in such an intricate fashion that it's hard to comprehend how the heart can pump, blood can flow, the lungs can breathe, the kidneys can flush, the intestines can digest, and the brain can coordinate all of the above. In fact, the brain (where Jason's tumor was) is remarkable in that it is responsible for instructing the body through all of the ins and outs of these various functions, all while exhibiting an ability to think critically about the details of the day and the problems presented before it. And most notably, the brain is not just capable of processing information about the world around it, but amazingly, it can objectively think about itself and the various functions it is performing all at the same time as it, indeed, performs.

This is to say that while human beings view disease as an aberration, God probably views disease much differently. He most likely sees it as living proof that healthy bodies that he, himself, designed are not only exceptional but wholly perfect. If only sin had not entered the world, what was perfect could have stayed that way.

Find your beach. Be patient. Let the body work—it's complex and amazingly designed.

Chapter 12

Beverly McKane

Jason was blessed to have numerous people in his life praying for him and showing him kindness on a regular basis. However, one person truly stood out as exceptionally inclined to devoting her time and effort to Jason's cause: Ms. Beverly McKane of Okemos, Michigan. Like the Merkles, she was a member at First Baptist Church of Okemos. Bev, as Jason called her, was a determined and compassionate individual. She worked at least two different jobs in the area—a position at the public library and performing laundry duties at the Douglas J. Salon. When Beverly needed to go somewhere, she walked or caught a ride with a friend. Because of her aversion to automobiles, she never owned or drove a car during her sixty-five years of life. Moreover, Bev admits proudly that she has lived in the same house that she grew up in many years ago. And why not? Bev adored her small-town home, and she had no desire to be anywhere else. When you meet with Beverly McKane, it feels like you are traveling back in time to a space when things were simpler and people were kinder and not always in such a hurry. One immediately feels at peace around her, which is a rare experience in the hustle and bustle of modern living.

When Beverly learned of Jason's illness, she immediately set to work to raise money for his cause. Over the course of the next several months, she established the Jason Merkle Foundation, a fund-raising initiative that collected donations in hundreds of money jars placed in the entryways of local businesses throughout the area, including the towns of Okemos and Williamston. Gas stations, grocery stores, salons, restaurants, and post offices all over the area solicited donations for Jason's cause. Jason's picture, along with a short description of his plight, was on each jar. Friends and fellow church members would drive Beverly to each location, and she would check the jars every few days to see how much money had been raised. Over the course of the next two years, Beverly raised a whopping seventeen thousand dollars for Jason's cause—a staggering amount of money considering many of those donating most likely had never met Beverly or Jason. Beverly explained, "I prayed much about the Jason Merkle Foundation. Over three hundred and fifty people came into the Douglas J. Salon each day alone, and people would leave cash and checks every day for Jason."

Jason and Beverly developed a great friendship during his illness. On days when Jason was feeling better and was able to drive, he would pick Bev up at her home, and they would go to lunch at nice restaurants such as the Golden Rose. "Everybody else was dating," said Beverly, "and he wasn't doing much of anything. I took him to lunch to bring up his spirits." Jason enjoyed these outings a great deal. They helped him get his mind off things, and the money Bev was raising for his cause always encouraged him and gave him hope.

On one occasion, she forced Jason into the mall and spent five hundred dollars on new clothes for him for his return to college. Jason describes Bev as a very difficult person to say no to, which is a great quality in a fund-raiser for sure, but it made it impossible for Jason not to accept Beverly's generosity. He spent several hours that day shopping and refreshing his wardrobe, as well as his mind and spirit. Beverly was helping Jason to keep focused on his future and his eventual recovery. It was days like that day when Jason could escape the monotony and dread of his battle with cancer. Each day he awoke searching for new hope, asking God to keep his spirits high. The greatest battle a person will face in his or her battle with cancer is in his or her own mind. If one allows the depression and dread to be pervasive, it will be a losing battle for the body; on the contrary, if one stays optimistic and maintains hope, stomping down the demons of despair, the body will have a better likelihood of recovery. Because of Bev's thoughtfulness and generosity, Jason found it easier to achieve a certain levity that kept his mind and body poised to do battle with its morbid foe. He could win, even against all odds, because Beverly McKane was tangible proof of God answering prayers in his time of need.

For Jason's twenty-first birthday, Beverly gave a special gift to Jason with which he thought she would never part—the key to Lansing, Michigan. Beverly's cousin, Terry McKane, who had been mayor of the city at one time, had given her the key many years earlier. But on this occasion, Beverly decided that Jason should have it. "He looked wiped out from his battle with brain cancer," Beverly said. "I thought maybe he was going to pass away. It's quite an honor to get a key like that. I prayed that God would somehow touch his body and that Jason would be a witness all the days of his life."

Beverly continued, "Jason is one of those people you want to cheer up," stated Beverly, "but instead he cheers you up." Even at his worst, according to Beverly, he still worked hard to carry a sunny disposition despite how he might be feeling inside.

"He left a real mark on my life," indicated Beverly. "We thought he was going to die, but God revealed that he really wants Jason around for a long time. Only eternity will reveal how many people have been touched by Jason. His faith was so strong for somebody so young."

Beverly made Jason's life a little easier during one of the most harrowing times of his life. The financial support would have been more than enough, but it was her friendship that most impacted Jason. While many people were tied up in the struggles of their individual lives, Beverly was tied up in Jason's, and that is a rare and unique characteristic that demonstrates the unselfishness of a committed disciple of Christ.

In one more tremendous act of kindness, Beverly escorted Jason to a professional photographer and had pictures taken for his parents. It was a genuine effort to capture the moment for his parents to cherish forever. Regardless of the outcome, they could always look back on these pictures with fondness, remembering the woman who worked so hard to brighten their family's world during the darkest of times.

Beverly went on to help others too. When a small six-year-old girl fell through the ice and nearly drowned, Beverly was there. Because of the tragic accident, Kate would need special care for the remainder of her life. She would never eat, walk, or talk again, but thanks to Beverly, large donations have been given to her and her family. Tragedies happen each and every day. Some of us withdraw in order to cope with them; some of us lie low, not knowing what to do. But Beverly McKane is the kind of person who takes action and lends a hand without asking for anything in return. Without question, she is the Lord's servant.

Finally, when asked about her overall impression of Jason Merkle through his trials, she said, "He is unusual." There was a long pause after she stated this, as if she was both expecting a follow-up question pleading for more specifics and was buying time to think of how to best clarify this description. She continued, "He is an unusual man who loves the Lord deeply. God is the center of his life. He wants to do what God wants him to do, and he is unusual because of his faith. And he really wants other people to come to know the Lord in a personal way."

It is unusual for a man of twenty or twenty-one years to have such a strong faith. But why is that so unusual? Most people expect older people to be more inclined to go to church or to pray regularly, but rarely is it seen as odd for a young person to be without faith. Because Jason solidified his faith in God at such a young age, he was emboldened by the certainty of his own eternity with the Lord. If one believes that, live or die, he or she has a future—a real future full of joy and hope and a plethora of good things—fear and dread inevitably recede. What Bev McKane and Jason Merkle share in common is a rock-solid faith in the Lord's plan for their lives, and God specifically brought them together during this time of their lives—one old and one young—to sharpen each other. Believers need other believers not so much because it makes faith in God easier to maintain—that would be the wrong way to put it—but because witnessing the Spirit of God in another person is proof of God's abundant love and grace for his Creation.

Let people help you and be generous to you. Swallow your pride. It is essential to your well-being and success.

Chapter 13

Elk Hunt and Dad's Journal

J ust when things seemed to be getting harder and harder, another great blessing came Jason's way. Dr. James Leonard, the president of Lansing Area Chapter Safari Club International (SCI), had learned about Jason's condition and approached Jason's dad, expressing their need for a Make a Wish candidate. The person chosen would go on a hunt sponsored by SCI. And so, they invited Jason to go on an elk hunt alongside a professional hunter. This was an opportunity that Jason could not pass up. Jason recalls feeling as sick as a dog when the doctor asked him to go on the adventure, but Jason had to go—the aspirations of a young man seeking a challenge could not be stifled by his deadly cancer. So he and his dad decided to go. The hunt would take place in February, and SCI would transport an elk from Canada onto the hunting grounds at a property called Deer Tracks in Michigan. Jason recalls that his vision and hearing were still largely impaired at this time. His condition was advanced now, and the likelihood of success in hunting in such a condition was not probable. Still, Jason pressed on with great determination.

Jay, the professional hunter who would accompany Jason and his dad on the elk hunt, proved to be very accommodating. Made aware of Jason's condition, he did everything he could to make the hunt comfortable for him. Professional hunters were always required to go on these kinds of hunts to be sure that the amateur hunters only shot and killed older animals. They did not want younger deer or fawns to be unnecessarily killed. Most of the deer on the property at this time would not have antlers, making it very difficult to discern older deer from younger deer. In fact, Jason did not know he was hunting an elk; he thought he was hunting a buck. It was not until Jason saw the elk through the scope that he realized the animal he was hunting was not a deer.

Jason remembers the day vividly:

> We were tracking the elk in eight inches of snow, and I was exhausted. My ears were ringing, and my vision was so bad that I could not even make out that it was an elk. But I could see through the scope of the gun okay. Jay, the professional, would get down on both knees and allow me to rest the gun on his shoulder. I could see the elk from a distance through the scope. I saw the elk from far away but did not have a shot as he ran away, possibly sensing danger. We went back to the cabin and had lunch and went back out in the afternoon. I caught sight of the elk through some trees, and I got down on one knee, and Jay got down on both knees, as I rested the gun on his shoulder. I fired, and down the elk went.

The God of the universe does not operate within the parameters of human probabilities or likelihood. Despite all the disadvantages Jason had in not being able to see or hear, like the feeble David of the Bible facing the formidable giant Goliath, Jason shot and killed an elk—an eight-hundred pounder! The importance of this animal's life was not lost on Jason or his family, as they all saw it as a sign of

God's provision for their family. The meat from that elk was pure and unprocessed, and since Jason's contraction of brain cancer, the family had made a point of not eating processed foods, which are riddled with cancer-producing agents. This elk meat would be savored and enjoyed by Jason's family, and they thanked God for this miracle. Moreover, the *Lansing State Journal* took particular interest in Jason's story and wrote a special piece on his condition and the success of the elk hunt. One cannot overestimate how much fatigue cancer patients experience by simply engaging in everyday activities. Hunting in the cold of February for most of the day would be hard on the average person, but for Jason it was especially difficult. His resolve was tested that day, and he never shrunk in the face of adversity. In Jason's mind, he would shoot an elk that day or die trying. On the way home from the hunt, Jason's dad recalls Jason falling into a deep sleep. Jason woke up suddenly, kicking the dashboard and startling his dad. "I had a dream about killing the elk," he recalls.

And the miracles just kept coming. At the end of February, Jason had an MRI that revealed that the tumor had shrunk by 20 percent! None of the doctors could effectively explain it except that the treatment must be working. Moreover, because of Jason's success on the elk hunt, Jason was invited by the chapter president to attend the Safari Club International banquet. He was called up on stage during the dinner, and out from behind stage, the head of the elk he had shot and killed was brought out for all to see—the taxidermist had completed the work in swift fashion. The presenter of the award shared some of Jason's story in his fight with cancer and shared a video of Jason shooting and killing the elk. The video and Jason's story especially touched two people in the audience. The first was a woman from Out of Africa, an exotic hunting ground in the heart of South Africa. She came up on stage and offered to donate a trip for Jason and his family to come and hunt. After Jason graciously accepted that invitation, a second man named Chuck Bazzy also offered to donate a trip on a hunting expedition in South Africa. Jason was blown away—there was clearly no escaping the Lord's plan for him to go to Africa. Jason recalls, "The Lord was telling me to go to Africa at one of the most inconvenient times of my life—when I was uncomfortably sick and fighting for my life." Even stranger for Jason and his family was the fact that people that they had never met were offering to make generous donations to Jason's cause. It was a sign that God truly calls people to love one another. Mark 12:30–31 states, "Love the Lord your God with all your heart and with all your soul and with all your mind and with all your strength.… Love your neighbor as yourself. There is no commandment greater than these."

A few days later more good news followed.

On March 8, 2002, Jason's tumor showed 16 percent more shrinkage, according to his father's journals. Dr. Burzynski was happy to report the good news to Jason's doctor, Dr. Jurrida. Jason's dad indicated in his journal, "We may have been pushing the limit with the FDA in terms of showing a response to the antineoplastons."

Here, Jason's father admits that there were tenuous moments between the FDA and the Burzynski Clinic. Apparently, the FDA had it out for the clinic despite its success.

March 19, 2002: "Jason is receiving cards from an anonymous person each day for a little over a week with a dollar in each card. Isn't it just like our God to provide encouragement each day through the unexpected and the unknown?"

March 23, 2002: "Jason threw up twice today. Jason had visitors from Cedarville: JoEllen, Casey and Sarah are so kind to Jason. He took them to Sahara's for lunch. Jason had a good day and did very well. We prayed tonight for God's continued hand of healing and the significance of this week leading up to Easter. There were articles about Jason in the Williamston Enterprise and the Lansing State Journal today." JoEllen was one of Jason's closest friends from Cedarville. She mailed him several cards and letters and even visited him on occasion in Williamston. Here is one of her letters to Jason.

> Well, you are back at home now. I am praying all is going well. How is it being home without your two younger brothers there? I know it is really weird to me going home and not having my little sister there.

How is everyone doing? I hope well! I pray for your family as much as I do you!! I have these next two weeks off in between summer school and fall quarter. I am so glad for a break. Well, I don't want to keep you long but I wanted to send a card to let you know I am praying for you and missing you. I can't wait to hear from you soon and find out how well the treatment is working. I hope to see you soon Jason. Me and Casey would love to come visit you if you are still at home next quarter. Can't wait to hear from you. Have a great day and please remember I am praying for you!

Jason was surrounded by an infantry of prayer specialists, including JoEllen. Church members and fellow Cedarville students alike formed a kind of protective wall around him during this time, battling death and despair as a Christian team united for one purpose—to watch God do the impossible for him, healing him not within the boundaries of science or medicine but from within the community of steadfast Christian believers. Several complete strangers, including people from Cedarville and the Williamston community, wrote to Jason. Here are some excerpts from their letters:

Dear Jason:

I know you don't know me, but I really wanted to write you. My name is Elizabeth, but I go by my middle name, Dawn. I am a freshman at Cedarville and am from Bellbrook, Ohio, which is about a half hour away from Cedarville. Anyway, I wanted to write you and tell you that I'm thinking and praying for you. We all are. I have heard a lot about you. I have heard about your strength through all this (and I even heard that you make great prank phone calls). I want you to know that you have been a witness and encouragement to me and many others. God is shining through you and raising you every day! Never forget how much God loves you and how much all of us at Cedarville love you.

Dear Jason:

We are so pleased for you in receiving the news concerning your treatment. We thank and praise our most sovereign God. We know he is very near you, his Holy Spirit continually filling you with his power, strength, love and encouragement. We are loving and caring for you and your family.

Jason!!!

I am Beverly McKane's friend, Sally. I want you to know that my parents, daughter and niece have been praying for your health and total healing. I have been praying too. It must be a drag to be so 'young and fun' and have to deal with all you are handling. I bet you desire to just be normal and live a normal life so often. I am sorry for this fact. You will have a lot more character than most people your age (and do already), but that does not make it easy or desirable. Know that strangers like me really do care about you. Imagine how much God cares.

Of all the people that loved and cared for Jason during his illness, Jason described the Four Horsemen as the most dedicated and enthusiastic of all. Who were the four horsemen? They were not men at all but four women who came to visit and stay with him on a regular basis during his illness. They were Lindsay, Sarah, JoEllen, and Casey. These four special ladies came on several occasions and stayed all weekend with Jason and his family, sleeping in the vacant rooms where Jason's brothers had once been before they left for college. During those visits, the four women encouraged Jason in his fight with cancer, and Jason describes them as incredibly compassionate people who knew that Jason needed a distraction from the chaos of his current plight. Whenever people outside one's family come around, a person tends to act differently than when he or she is with family alone. There is something in the human condition that causes people to be on their best behavior with those outside of immediate family. So while they stayed, even though Jason was tough and strong-willed, these ladies helped Jason be even stronger during these weekend visits. After all, a man wants to do his best and look his best around four attractive ladies. Jason said he called these ladies the Four Horseman because they came often and always came together. Like the four horsemen in the Book of Revelation, they had a purpose, and their purpose was a divine calling to cheer a friend who was suffering greatly. May God bless those who serve others during tribulation and pain.

Two other people who were there for Jason at this time were his older brother, Dan, and his cousin, Andy. Dan lived closest to home of all of Jason's brothers, so they spent a great deal of time together during his illness. Jason and Dan went to movies, out to dinner, and even to sporting events when Jason was feeling well enough. On one occasion at the movie theater, Jason was so fatigued from his meds that he fell asleep during the movie. "Dan helped me keep a good sense of humor and took my mind off of things. He also helped me by pushing me harder in the day-to-day fight."

Likewise, Jason's cousin Andy spent a lot of time with Jason during this period. Jason and Andy got together once a week to have dinner and watch *Survivor*, the hit TV show. The significance of the title of the TV program was not lost on Jason. He, too, saw himself as a survivor, and the tribulations of the characters on the show paralleled his own. The TV program's plot line captivated its audiences on how and when people would give up living in perilous conditions. The last person standing would win the prize. In his own battle, Jason knew that he would have to continue to suffer seemingly unbearable conditions to conquer the nemesis in his own body.

While Jason's tumor had shrunk during this period, his trials and tribulations seemed to never end. He was still very sick, and there was no guarantee that he would survive. Dr. Jurrida—the Burzynski specialist who examined the MRI each month to assess Jason's progress—candidly explained to the family that Jason's hope for survival had greatly increased, but he was certainly not out of the woods yet. As the next few months progressed, Jason would have to stay steadfast in the antineoplaston treatment and continue to suffer through the excessive vomiting and lack of sleep. Dr. Jurrida estimated that it could take eight to fourteen months for the tumor to completely disappear.

For the next several months, Jason wrestled with the cancer, as it seemingly fought to maintain its stranglehold on Jason's life. As if it was a living force in and of itself, the malignancy in Jason's brain was not going to give up without declaring war on Jason's life. Although he had already endured so much, this cancer would prove not to be merely a dispensable foe. It kept coming at him like a raging lion desperate for food. Like Jason, the cancer wanted to live, but in the process, it had to kill its host. And so, day-to-day living was increasingly difficult as Jason struggled to regain his strength. His father made journal entries each and every day from August 2001 throughout the entire year of 2002, diligently tracking Jason's dosages of medicine and his progress. What follows are the highlights of April and May of 2002.

> April 7, 2002: "Jason did not feel well today. His massage yesterday was not helpful. His neck, shoulders, and arms are all very sore. He feels miserable. We are going to take him off treatment tonight—he has thrown up twice tonight. It seems we can only go about a week at a time before we take him off treatment for a few doses. He is dizzy again. Lord, give us wisdom to evaluate the situation!"

> April 26, 2002: "We received a report from the
> Burzynski Clinic that Jason's tumor had grown around
> 10 percent. Dr. Jurrida shared that the condition was
> not unusual. Although we were quite disappointed,
> Jason ended the day tired but certainly gaining
> strength."

Almost two months prior, Jason and his family had been given the news that the tumor had begun shrinking for the first time. As March came to a close, Dr. Jurrida had indicated that the odds were now in Jason's favor for survival and that the tumor could be completely gone in eight to fourteen months. Now, even though Dr. Jurrida had stated that the tumor's rebound was not unusual, it made it incredibly hard to keep going. The menacing metaphor of taking two steps forward only to take one step back became so real for the Merkle family at this time. Each time they received encouraging news, they were battered about with equally discouraging setbacks.

Around this time, the local community and the First Baptist Church of Okemos put on an auction of goods and tickets to sporting events to raise money for Jason's cause. Several people and local businesses donated to the event to be auctioned off in support of Jason.

> April 27, 2002: "Jason woke up feeling strong. He
> did two miles on the stairs. We had just a super day.
> God was so good. The auction raised approximately
> $17,500. Jason shared briefly at the auction. God has
> provided once again and reminded us of his love for
> us. God is so good."

Throughout Jason's sickness, his church and community worked to raise money to support Jason's family in the face of excessively high medical expenses. The antineoplaston treatment cost sixteen thousand dollars per month! Despite medical insurance paying for MRIs and blood work, the Merkles were saddled with the cost of the treatment, which amounted to two hundred thousand dollars per year when all of the additional, miscellaneous expenditures were factored in.

April 29, 2002: "Jason drove into town alone today and is tired and napped before dinner. We all went to Kmart after dinner tonight. We picked up a couple of things for the safari. We are concerned but are trusting God for reduction in the tumor—no, not reduction, but total elimination of Jason's tumor."

May 2, 2002: "Jason had lunch with John and Ashley. Jason then rode in with Josh to pick up a few things in town. Jason failed to bring enough water and did not pick up any. When he got home, he was tired and took a two-hour nap. He soon ate around seven o'clock. He started to feel bad and realized he had not had enough water. He began throwing up around eight fifteen. He threw up several times until around 11:00. We finally were able to calm his system down enough to take a few pills and drink a little water. When his sodium gets high, he becomes very sick to his stomach."

May 4, 2002: "Jason had a good day. He went with Jordan to the driving range and also to the batting cage. He also exercised today."

May 5, 2002: "Jason had nine friends from Cedarville visit at church and then lunch at Old Country Buffet."

As mentioned before, Jason's treatment cost nearly sixteen thousand dollars a month—an outrageous amount for any middle-class family that has two other boys in college. Contributing to Jason's cause was the Cedarville student body, tithing each week in Jason's name, along with donations from several local churches in Jason's area, including Williamston Free Methodist. Also, two young ladies, Molly and Beth, from Jason's high school graduating class in 1999 raised several thousands of dollars by sending out donation letters to high school kids and their families. All in all, Jason had support from so many across the community in Williamston and in Cedarville.

> May 6 and 7, 2002: "Jason and Patty are at Cedarville today."

> May 11, 2002: "Josh, Matt, and Seth came up from Cedarville today, and it was good to see them. We grilled out and had elk burgers for an afternoon lunch. Jason was very tired today and seems to be having a hard time."

> May 12, 2002: "Jason is struggling today with his medication. He has started to throw up again; we feel that he has thrown up so many times that he might not be able to digest food normally. This has been a very long road, and we all are becoming weary. Please help us Lord as we work through these times and give us the strength to be a light to those in need. Happy Mother's Day! We all ate out at Sahara's except Jason."

> May 14, 2002: "Jason is having a hard time keeping going. He is not back to his normal self."

> May 15, 2002: "Jason is much stronger today. We picked Jonathan up from college today. Both boys are home, and it sure is nice."

> May 19, 2002: "Jason had a pretty good day. He threw up tonight and choked on a pill. He seems to do far better eating smaller amounts more often."

May 21, 2002: "Jason played a little soccer with Jonathan and Jordan. Jason prayed for divine healing and for the tumor to be removed. We all prayed asking God for a miracle in providing healing and for your grace and faithfulness. Patty read Psalm 9:14: 'Because he loves me, says the Lord, I will rescue him. I will protect him, for he acknowledges my name. He will call upon me, and I will answer him; I will be with him in trouble, I will deliver him and honor him. With long life will I satisfy him and show him my salvation.'"

May 24, 2002: "Jason is feeling pretty good. We received word that the MRI showed Jason's tumor is smaller! Thank you Lord!"

Despite all his trials and tribulations, Jason always managed to have a little fun. Ping-pong was one of his favorite activities with friends. Even in his sickly state, Jason Merkle was one of the most competitive people that God so wonderfully crafted with his own two hands. Several times through the spring and summer of 2002, Jason would taunt his friends Jason V. and Ryan as he pummeled them in ping-pong matches. He would chant, "Come on, guys, I am legally blind. How can you lose to a legally blind cancer patient?" At one point, Ryan became so angry that he slammed his brand new paddle over his knee, breaking it in two, after having become incensed by Jason's antics as he lost yet another match to his disabled friend.

As the losses piled up, Jason V., in fact, became so enraged that he challenged Jason to a foot race. In the past, Jason had always been faster than his friend, Jason V., but the latter thought for sure that he could finally beat Jason in his dilapidated condition. Jason, who was a born competitor, accepted the challenge. As they took off running, Jason kept pace with Jason V. for the first part of the race but then stumbled and fell, losing the race to his friend, who was elated beyond expression. As Jason V. celebrated, Jason picked himself up, wiped some of the dirt from his clothes, and simply said, "Congratulations. You just beat my cancer, and so will I."

Make a wish! Spend some time away from modern technology. Have someone document everything for you. Embrace kindness and stay motivated.

Chapter 14

The Atheist

I n the spring of 2002, Jason received an unlikely request. An atheist teacher—we will call her Ms. White for the sake of anonymity— from Jason's old high school asked Jason to come speak about the American dream to her students. Jason accepted the request, never denying an opportunity to share with others, but he was unaware at the time that Ms. White was an atheist. When one of the school administrators informed him of this fact, Jason was undaunted. After all, it was doubtful that Ms. White was unaware herself of Jason's religious background, as he was very nearly a celebrity in Williamston and in the surrounding area. Surely, she had read about Jason and researched his background before inviting him to her class. And even if this was not the case, Jason not only saw this as an opportunity to encourage young people in the face of trials, but moreover, he saw this as an opportunity to serve as a witness for the good news of Jesus Christ. In short, Jason was unashamed of his beliefs, and he certainly would not be shaken by someone who disagreed with him, even if he or she was a respected teacher in the community.

Jason arrived that day carrying his fanny pack filled with a sufficient supply of medicine for the day. He also brought a couple of gallons of water, which he drank on a regular basis to flush the sodium from his system. In short, Jason was an odd sight to your average high school student as he sat perched on a stool with his pack and his port, drinking water at unusually short intervals while he spoke. To counteract the electrolytes that he was flushing from his system—that is, sodium, potassium, magnesium, and calcium—Jason would also take several vitamins throughout the day to replenish his system with three out of the four electrolytes, sodium excluded. So Jason will tell you he was a pill-popping, water-guzzling, antineoplaston-pumping machine throughout the day as he proclaimed his testimony to six different classes.

Of course, none of that mattered to Jason. He was fearless and unabashed in his less-than-ideal state of existence. Over the course of the morning and afternoon, Jason shared his testimony (which he was still in the midst of, by the way) with close to one hundred students. The most important part of his testimony, of course, was his description of the ultimate source of his strength and endurance during this challenging time. Jason explained that he cast all his cares upon the Lord as he held up a Bible in his hand—he knew that the Lord cared for and loved him deeply and would bring him through these tribulations according to his great power and wisdom. He went on to say that while he had normal human fears, God had sustained him throughout this process, quelling those fears and anxieties as he faced the impossible—the formidable foe that is deadly brain stem cancer. "With God all things are possible," asserted Jason, quoting Matthew 19:26.

To Jason's astonishment, Ms. White never interrupted him with atheistic protestations against his biblical references. In fact, he never looked over to see Ms. White's reaction as he expressed his Christian beliefs in a bold and unabated fashion. He simply looked the students in the eyes and saw that they were paying attention, and he prayed that God's word would be heard through his testimony. Ms. White was kind throughout the day to Jason and even paid for his lunch. And it's not as if Jason did not expect kindness from an atheist; it's that he didn't expect there not to be a confrontation. However, perhaps Ms. White was curious herself how such a young man with such a degenerative disease, facing overwhelming odds, seemed to not only be managing it all so graciously but, what's more, seemingly winning the race!

Each class ended with applause followed by several questions from students. Again, young Jason exhausted himself in service of the Lord, not hesitating to share what God had done for him. This young man, who appeared quite sickly and had a couple of gallons of water accompanying his intravenous fanny pack, was simultaneously frightening and enlightening to students that day. Here was a man facing the worst of all diseases and testifying to the greatness of God in the midst of it! The Lord had hand-picked Jason to be his faithful witness because he was obedient even in the midst of—especially in the midst of—great adversity.

Jason left his high school that day pondering the years of his life spent there that had been so carefree. Truly, high school had been the time of his life in between brain surgery and the cancer diagnosis. He could not help but be nostalgic for a few moments, but then it was time to move on to face the beast. Regardless of how easy that time had been in his life, this was the time in his life that was molding and sculpting him to endure life's hardships and struggles. *It will get easy again*, he thought, *but for now, I am in God's boot camp, so to speak, where I am being trained to be a warrior for God's kingdom.*

Several students who heard Jason's talk wrote him letters, thanking him for his courage to share his vulnerability and his testimony to having a good attitude in the face of extreme adversity. What follows is a sampling of the letters Jason received:

Dear Jason,

I think it's inspiring to hear someone that went through some tough times and still have a strong faith in God. You know He can help you through anything. Thank you again for coming to talk to us.

–Esther

Dear Jason,

What you said about not giving up and relying on God really inspired me to not give up. During this past Summer my brother was also diagnosed with cancer in his arm. I prayed a lot and after his second surgery, the cancer was gone.

–Drew

Dear Jason,

I've recently had an aunt be diagnosed with cancer. She has a growth around her heart. She is able to walk and talk now, but unfortunately has to wear a wig because her hair is falling out. I now have more hope for her from hearing of your personal experiences. You are truly a miracle and deserve to live a long, happy life.

–Alaina

Jason,

It was nice to hear how your faith in God helps carry you through hard times. God has helped me through hard times too. Take care and I will pray for you and your ministry.

–Chris

Dear Jason,

Although I don't entirely agree with your religious and
lifestyle views. I appreciate that you came in to talk
to us. I hope everything works out for you and you
become the shining image of health soon.

–Ben

In all, Jason touched students who believed in the Lord and those
who had no faith at all through his story. God was using Jason to
tell people about his son, Jesus. And Jesus, probably being the most
controversial person in world history, was using a strong believer like
Jason to explain that the struggles of life are unavoidable but that God
has a glorious plan for all people who turn to him during and in spite
of tribulation. The Bible in 1 Corinthians 2:9 states, "What no eye
has seen, nor ear has heard, nor the heart of man imagined, what
God has prepared for those who love him." God had used an atheist
to give him a platform to speak about God's magnificent work in his
own life. Either the Lord has a tremendous appreciation for irony,
or he wants to have a relationship with all his people, regardless of
background or religious inclination.

*Differences happen. Don't judge. Love and kindness can overcome.
Share your story with others. Live a life of purpose.*

Chapter 15

South Africa

O ver the next month or so in June 2002, the Merkle family prepared for their safari in Africa. While Jason was greatly looking forward to the trip, he also experienced a sense of fear in going to such a foreign continent—the land that God had called him toward just five years ago. What's more, Jason was still sick, and the family had to prepare for a long plane ride as well as missing the conveniences of American life. It was yet to be seen how Jason's body would respond to the African climate, not to mention the long travel time.

In July 2002, the Merkle family traveled to South Africa together, which was paid for by the fund-raising of Safari Club International. To have an expense-free vacation such as this one was a blessing that could not be overstated. Upon arrival at the airport, the Merkle family received yet another blessing—the airline informed them that they were being bumped up to first class. One way or another, the airline had received word about Jason's condition and decided that they would not only upgrade the family to more comfortable seating on the eighteen-hour flight to Johannesburg, Africa, but would also give them premium access to their frequent flyers club during the layover in New York. The Merkles were humbled by such a gracious offer; the upgrade allowed them to enjoy the privileges of gourmet food and a spa treatment during their wait.

The Merkles first arrived in Johannesburg, where they then caught a connecting flight to St. Petersburg. There they met Hank and Sariette, who transported them to the outpost about two hours away—called Out of Africa—a destination situated far away from civilization in what Africans call the bush. At the outpost, they slept in small twelve-feet-by-ten-feet huts. Jason had his own hut, and his parents had their own. Over the course of the trip, the Burzynski Clinic required that Jason complete his blood work and urine work every other day. On those days, a driver had to transport Jason's samples back to St. Petersburg for transfer to the clinic in Houston, Texas. To say nothing of their current status in being outside the comforts of home on a completely different continent, the Merkles possessed a deeply rooted faith in God's sovereignty and his desire for them to trust him and only him during this trial. While many people, including those in the clinic, might consider the Merkles' trip risky and unnecessarily laborious, the family saw it as an opportunity to grow as people and disciples of Jesus Christ.

On day one of the trip, Jason and his family met with CJ, a professional hunter, and Pete, the assistant and animal tracker. They drove about an hour into the wilderness and saw all kinds of wild, exotic animals, including giraffes, gazelle, blue wildebeests, impalas, anteaters, warthogs and zebras. They spent all day viewing the animals and arrived back at camp in the early evening.

The next day Jason had his first opportunity to hunt. That day, he shot an eight-hundred-pound kudu; two days later, Jason targeted a zebra, a warthog, and an impala, killing each of them with one shot. All of the meat from the animals was donated to local villages where the less fortunate resided. In the evenings, all the people at the outpost ate dinner together and discussed the adventures of the day. This was a memorable time, meeting people from all over the world who had come together for different reasons, perhaps, but with just one simple objective: to hunt and kill.

During their time in Out of Africa, Jason developed a strong relationship with the professional hunter assigned to him—CJ, or JC. He told Jason that he could call him by either name. This name struck Jason as fortuitous since Jesus is often referred to as Christ Jesus or Jesus Christ in the Bible. The initials of his guide were the same as Jesus' initials, and Jason saw it as a sign that God was blessing this expedition in the middle of an unknown wilderness. CJ was incredibly confident and unafraid—he led Jason and his family through the wilderness with unabated resolve and skillful planning. Without CJ, the family would have been lost or even devoured by wild animals, much like people in the world can be when striving to live their lives without the knowledge or guidance of the Lord.

Moreover, Jason's time with Pete, the South African tracker, was very impactful. While greatly skilled and incredibly joyful in his duties, Pete was very poor. Jason and Pete, both about the same age, became quick friends, and Pete taught Jason a great deal about the inhabitants and wildlife in South Africa. In the short time that Jason and Pete were together, they became close friends—so much so that Jason decided to leave most of his possessions with Pete, with the exception of the clothes he needed for the rest of the trip. Jason explained that he felt called to serve Pete, and the best way he felt like he could do that was by offering him some of his precious possessions. Jason could always buy more clothes, shoes, hats, books, and gadgets, whereas for Pete, an opportunity to possess such things was outside the realm of his reality. Charles Spurgeon, a Christian thinker and theologian, states, "It is great privilege to exhaust ourselves in service of the Lord." Jason was, indeed, exhausted during this trip, but the Lord gave him strength to endure each and every day. His condition was not ideal for a safari in Africa, for an elk hunt in Michigan, or even for ministering to others in a land not his own, but Jason did all those things with the help of God Almighty.

The first part of the trip came to an end, and Jason and his family traveled back to St. Petersburg for the second leg of their trip, where they would meet with Chuck Bazzy, the second donor to Jason's cause. Chuck decided to take them camping in a national park nearby, where they spent two nights in pitched tents. That evening, while the Merkles slept in their tents outside in the wilderness, Jay Merkle described the experience as quite "primitive in nature," as lions were heard roaring in the distance. Jason's mother was terrified. Two armed guards kept watch over the campgrounds during the night, and all the tents surrounded a large campfire in an effort to keep large cats from entering the grounds. Lions, and most cats in general, are nocturnal and spend a significant part of their nights seeking out food. This was a much different experience from their time in Out of Africa, as they were literally planted in the wilderness near what Chuck described as "the big five"—that is, the hippo, rhino, elephant, leopard, and lion. Chuck told Jason, "Tomorrow you are going to dart one of the big five for observational and tracking purposes." In an effort to crack down on poachers, many of these large animals were tagged and tracked so that law enforcement could find and target people who were abusing the hunting laws and killing these animals for unlawful monetary gain—in many cases, the sale of ivory from tusks and horns.

The next day, Chuck, a professional hunter, a veterinarian, and Jason's family began searching for a rhinoceros to dart and tag. About the middle of the day, they found one that had not yet been tagged. Jason approached the rhino from a distance, took aim, and fired the gun, but when the dart on the tranquilizer hit the rhino, it did not go through the animal's tough skin! Hurrying Jason back to the truck, the professional hunter warned everyone that this may have angered the rhino, and so they had Jason line up his next shot from the bed of the truck. He aimed and fired—it was a direct hit! As the rhino began to grow weary, the team moved in and tied ropes around the animal's legs to help it fall and land on the ground safely. Oftentimes, the animals will fall awkwardly, breaking their legs and rendering them useless for the remainder of their lives. So the team had to take extreme precaution to help the process go smoothly and preserve the health of the rhino. Finally, the rhino toppled to the ground unconscious, and the team poured water over the rhino to keep it cool in the hot sun while they worked to tag it. They drilled small holes into its horns in order to place microchips inside, allowing the team to determine the source of the ivory if it was confiscated after the animal had been poached.

For a hunter like Jason, this was quite the experience. He, too, was being hunted by disease and death, much like the big five were being hunted and poached. It took creative methods to crack down on poachers, just as it took creative methods to beat a brain tumor. Of course, in order for future animals to survive, this rhino might give its life as a sacrifice. As more and more poachers get caught in the act of unnecessarily killing animals, fewer and fewer animals will become endangered.

The truth is that life is not the utopia that so many Westerners frame in their minds as an achievable reality. Regardless of the technological advances in medicine and the rise of civilization as protection from outside dangers, the hard truth of life is that everyone lives in a world represented well by the wilderness in which these animals live. Each day, it is a quest for survival. Some people must avoid being hunted and killed by disease and natural disasters; some people are killed every day by planes, trains, and automobiles; and some people die from the absence of clean water or even starvation. Within the warm nest called the civilized world, people have extended life and improved the quality within, but the reality of the world is that natural disasters cannot be prevented, tragic accidents will always occur, and it will never be the case that all diseases are cured. All people are hunted, in one way or another, on a regular basis by a foe called death, and the only hope for a life without death lies in the promise of Jesus Christ to be with him in Paradise, where neither animal nor human will be hunted any longer.

In all, Jason's South African safari was much different from the trip that he expected the Lord was calling him toward in 1997, just five years prior. From Jason's point of view, God was calling him to go to Africa to do mission work; instead, God used the once-in-a-lifetime adventure as a mission to heal Jason's own body and spirit. The timing could not have been better for Jason and his family. Worn out from the routine of endless cancer treatments, weary nights, and constant doctor's appointments and assessments, the Merkle family was sent out into the wild arena of the African continent, considered by many to be the continent on which primitive mankind first dwelled, including Adam and Eve and their descendants. It was here that Jason had the opportunity to tap into his natural masculine desires for adventure and even danger.

In truth, the safari was a different quest altogether for Jason. It was similar to the mission of Jonah when God calls him to go to Nineveh to warn the people of God's coming judgment. Unwilling and afraid, Jonah shrinks from the task and ends up on a ship headed for Tarshish. Because of his disobedience, Jonah is tossed into the sea by his shipmates and swallowed by a fish. It is here that Jonah comes to terms with his fear of the Lord, knowing full well that God's provision (the fish), while formidable, had saved him from drowning at sea. Jonah learned he must trust God in the calling of his life to Nineveh for preaching God's word.

Jason's journey was very similar to Jonah's in that he was afraid to go to Africa because of its distinct foreignness. Instead, Jason journeyed a different path, and his brain tumor paralleled that of the treacherous waters of the sea, sure to kill any man with its fury. But Jason's provision, like Jonah's fish, came in the form of an oversized bladder, a nonconventional cancer treatment, and the thousands of prayers from family members, friends, and strangers alike. And now, like it or not, at the behest of a total stranger's generosity, God had led him right into the heart of the place he feared and resisted most.

Returning from the African trip, Jason felt accomplished. Not only was his confrontation with African wildlife exactly what he needed to renew his mind and his spirit, it was also about fulfilling God's call for him to go to Africa. It would have been easy for Jason and his family to turn down the trip, especially when considering the inconveniences of antineoplaston treatment in the middle of the African wilderness. It seemed extreme to say the least to even take on such a harrowing adventure with Jason's state of health being so unpredictable. However, they had once again put their trust in the Lord to carry them through the journey, perhaps easing the burden of living with deadly cancer while on their travels. The greatest irony of all appeared in this mind-boggling fact: Jason's blood work results were better in Africa than at any other time during his treatment. Was this God showing his favor on Jason's finally making the trek to Africa, even if it was not on a mission trip, or was it simply because of an even healthier diet in Africa? Perhaps it was both. As Jay Merkle admitted, "We thought for a brief instant about keeping Jason in Africa for his treatment, but in the end, it would have proved too tedious." Still though, the blood work results were hard to dispute.

Don't run from your fears. Let God use you wherever you go. Don't be afraid to step outside of your comfort zone.

Jason with Pete with a kudu.

Jason with Chuck after tranquilizing a rhino.

Jason with CJ or JC with a warthog.

Chapter 16

Answered Prayer

Reality set in again as the Merkle family returned home from their expedition. Jason's struggles continued, as he battled stomach pains, vomiting, and weakness. Jason's dad admits that despite his son's not always feeling well, it was a challenge to find things for Jason to do to occupy his mind and body. Sometimes, he would ride his bike, and sometimes he would watch sports on television or listen to chapel services at Cedarville. But his inability to resume continuous, steady activity jilted Jason's sense of purpose. Jason had never been a couch potato or someone inclined to laziness, but this sickness had ushered in a routine of involuntary indolence on a regular basis. This was, indeed, maddening to the mind of an active twenty-one year old. Even if his body was incapable, his spirit craved the ability to live actively.

On August 15, the Merkle family received good news that the preliminary MRI seemed to show that the tumor had shrunk again slightly. Despite the back-and-forth battle with the tumor, incessant prayer combined with antineoplaston treatment seemed to be working. Jason had spent so much time with the MRI technician over the last several months that he was privileged enough to get a sneak peek at the images before the Burzynski Clinic called with the results. The waiting game was a difficult one, especially when one was forced to do so multiple times over the course of the year. It was these small acts of kindness that continued to encourage Jason.

In spite of the encouraging news for Jason, Jay and Patty attended the funeral of a friend who had just passed away after losing a battle with cancer. The Merkles had pushed their friend, Mike, to refrain from debilitating chemotherapy and radiation treatment, but Mike had decided not to do so. In the end, Jason's path required the patient to fight a longer battle and required greater sacrifice in terms of actual lifestyle change—the commitment to eating unprocessed foods and drinking large amounts of water.

It was disheartening for Jay and Patty to watch their friend pass of the same deadly disease with which their son was battling. Embittered, gut-wrenching thoughts crept into their minds of soon having to bury one of their own sons. Would Jason pull through despite all the odds stacked against him, and at what point would they possibly be forced to resign themselves to Jason's inevitable death? Surely God would not allow Jason to die after such a courageous and long struggle. Yet, reality was what it was—even though Jason was showing signs of improvement, brain cancer is as ruthless as it is volatile. At any moment, it could return in full force and crush all their hopes.

The next day, August 16, Dr. Jurrida called with the official results of the MRI. The tumor had shrunk a stunning 47 percent! The results were simply remarkable—this was the greatest shrinkage of the tumor since the time of diagnosis. Up until this point, the tumor's shrinkage had been relatively minimal. Now, however, incredible progress had been made. Dr. Jurrida told Jason's parents that they should try to help him gain some weight now to strengthen his body for the throes ahead. It was comparable to a general winning a great battle and pursuing the fleeing enemy. They should push forward now and try to crush the cancer with great resolve.

Ten days later, more tribulation followed victory. Jason's blood work indicated that his liver was greatly inflamed. The results indicated that it could possibly be due to a parasite picked up in South Africa. Moreover, Jason had been throwing up profusely since their return from Africa and now was also experiencing diarrhea. His life was utterly miserable at the moment, and his mom and dad felt overwhelmed with helplessness.

That evening, on August 26, 2002, they received a call from a man who had heard about Jason's case in South Africa who was donating money to his cause. Jason was in the midst of violent vomiting when the phone call came, so the timing could not have been better to help Jason's family keep hope alive. They disconnected Jason from treatment that evening to allow him to rest and hopefully allow time for his body to recover.

The next day, Jason's condition did not improve. His family doctor advised an ultrasound to check for gall bladder stones, so they set an appointment for 5:30 a.m. the next day. Jason's dad recorded in his journal, "Sometimes you have to play along just to keep the peace."

The following day, Jay continued his journal: "Jason had a very good day. We were at the hospital at 5:15 a.m. this morning for the ultrasound and the blood work. We stopped at McDonald's for breakfast at Jason's insistence to have a double egg bagel. He had two of these."

This is an interesting moment to note, as Jason generally would not eat fast food or any processed food altogether. Here, however, Jay sensed his son's need for a break from the dreaded monotony for an opportunity to feel normal again. Something as simple as two McDonald's double egg bagels provided a break from the chaos of a rugged routine.

Two days later, Jason's dad indicated in his journal that Jason had gained thirty pounds after being off the medication for about a week, which was good news in terms of Jason's overall strength. However, it was determined from the ultrasound that Jason had contracted a rotavirus while in South Africa. Without rest and proper care, the virus could result in a critical condition for Jason. Jason's dad wrote, "We are concerned about the situation, but we have to put this in God's hands with the confidence that he will finish the good work that he has begun."

In the days that followed, Jason continued to fight against the rotavirus, which resulted in intense and frequent vomiting and continued low energy. It was even discovered during this time that Jason had three dislocated ribs, probably due to the intense vomiting.

Several days later, Jason had yet another MRI. At this point, receiving the results became similar to getting a report card—simultaneously dreaded and highly anticipated. Jason's dad recorded this on October 9:

> Jason had an MRI today. Patty, Jason. and I looked at the scans but cannot see any enhancement around the tumor—in fact, we could not even pick out the tumor. We just don't know what to think but God is so in control.

The next day the official results were in: "We heard from Dr. Jurrida today. The tumor is 15 percent smaller in diameter and 10 percent shorter in length. Praise the Lord!" Getting this kind of news was exhilarating for the family. All their hard work and prayers were paying off in impressive form. Jason was slowly defeating one of the deadliest diseases on the planet with the help of the Lord Almighty. How precious were these moments when good news was received after months and months of misery and struggle, and all while watching the tumor grow from the size of a pinky tip to the size of a golf ball! Now, the tumor was smaller than the size of a fingertip! And what's more, it started to show in Jason's behavior over the next month. He began to engage in more active things such as racquetball and music concerts. The tide had finally started to turn for Jason, and Dr. Jurrida's prognosis now was that Jason would more than likely survive.

And in December 2002, sensational news arrived in the form of a phone call from the radiologist. Here is the way Jay Merkle described the next two days:

> December 4, 2002: "Jason had an MRI today. The preliminary report is very positive, showing more

tumor shrinkage as well as minor contrast with the
fourth ventricle now returning to normal size with the
radiologist being unable to measure the tumor, which
is now smaller than we first found it eight years ago."

December 5, 2002: "Jason is doing very good today.
We are praising the Lord for the good report from
the Burzynski Clinic. Dr. Jurrida called and said that
there was a problem. He said that they could not see
the tumor! Praise God! We will need to do a PET
scan and stay on the medicine for another three to
four months. We celebrated with Jason by going to
Chili's for dinner."

In December 2002, one year from the time he was hospitalized
with a staph infection that resulted in a skyrocketing body temperature
and a failing liver, Jason's tumor was completely gone. Over the last
several months, it had continued to reduce in size, but never did any
of the doctors expect it to recede completely into oblivion.

Just one year earlier, Jason's brother had prayed specifically and
unexpectedly for his brother to be completely healed in one year,
and God heard and answered this bold and mighty prayer. While
the person saying the prayer did not necessarily know or appreciate
the magnificence of God's healing power, the God of the Bible
responded with grace to let the entire family know that not only was
he listening, but he was interceding on Jason's behalf. Jason's very
name means "healer," which some will call a mere coincidence, but
can it be a coincidence when godly parents choose a name inspired
by God? Can it be a coincidence that Jason was healed exactly one
year from his brother's prayer? All the odds were against Jason. He
had the deadliest cancer known to man—a malignant tumor in
his brain stem that was inoperable. In the eyes of most doctors and
oncologists, Jason's situation was undoubtedly hopeless. His inevitable
fate could only be delayed, not altered. However, as Norman Vincent
Peale states in his book *The Power of Positive Thinking*, "Spiritual law

also governs illness. God has arranged two remedies for all illness. One is healing through natural laws applicable by science, and the other brings healing by spiritual law applicable through faith." This statement is especially applicable in Jason's case, as incessant prayers from family, friends, and strangers alike had served to guide Jason through the arduous and painstaking journey of brain cancer, which had not only tried Jason physically but had driven him into the depths of his very soul to discover how strong he could be in the face of the great adversary. His perseverance and willpower are rare to find in any individual, but his good humor and positive outlook in spite of the physical and spiritual misery he had endured over the last sixteen months were exceptional beyond comprehension.

Jason's uncle Van said this of Jason's journey: "Jason is disciplined and very driven. He is a man of strong character. In my mind, God's plan for us is not to be out of pain but to serve him and grow. God can use our situations, as he did for Jason. Jason knows that God has a purpose for him. His acts of living on a very strict diet and staying positive in the face of ultimate adversity show obedience, and his obedience led to an unlikely remission."

With God all things are possible. Be willing to take the road less traveled. You may lose some small battles, but press on to win the war!

Chapter 17

The Return of the Tumor

Although Jason's tumor was effectively gone, Jason was to remain on the treatment for several more months before finally going to a pill form of the antineoplaston drug. In January 2003, all was going smoothly, and Jason was once again thinking about his future—finishing up where he left off at Cedarville University and eventually pursuing his career. But yet another hiccup came just sixteen days into the new year. Dr. Jurrida called to report that the latest MRI showed a 20 to 30 percent resurgence of the tumor! Needless to say, Jason and his family felt both flabbergasted and deflated simultaneously. How could this be when just one month earlier the tumor was invisible? Had it been the excess of juice that Jason had been consuming? In the past, when Jason consumed largely acidic foods and drinks, tumor growth followed. Regardless, the news was maddening. It seemed that every time the tumor shrunk for a while, it came back in full force. Would there ever be a time when he could regain a normal livelihood?

It is during times like these that doubt begins to fester in the human heart and mind. So many times in life, progress is followed by a detrimental and deflating regression. In this case, it finally seemed that after eighteen months of misery, Jason could resume a normal life. How could it be that the tumor, after consistently diminishing over the last several months, could all of a sudden be resurging? After this long period of battling the cancer, fighting it with alternative treatment, a healthy diet, and most of all prayer, this was a cruel return to heartbreaking reality. The Merkles were weary and even despondent at this moment. Would they have the energy and strength to do battle with the nefarious tumor again? After all, they had just returned from battle in which the enemy was finally on the run. Bloodied and battered from the field, they did not see how they could go to war yet again, and even though it may not be the case, it seemed like they were starting all over again.

Over the next two days, the Merkle family returned to fervent prayer, asking the Lord for guidance, strength, and healing. They even petitioned God for an answer on why he had brought them this far in the journey, bringing them to the absolute threshold of a real miracle, only to watch it slip away. For two days, it was quiet around the household. Although everybody carried on with their lives as normally as possible, everyone felt a degree of apprehension and fear. Jason began to think about a full-blown return to sickness. He went back on a very strict diet, devoid of sugar and processed foods. He consumed many vegetables and alkaline-rich foods during this time, and there was a sense of guilt that came over him for daring to drink orange juice or even a soda now and then. While the rest of the world ingested and enjoyed juices, sodas, desserts, and delicious foods like pizza, cheeseburgers, and French fries, Jason was stripped of this opportunity not just by the desire to be well but by the guilt of feeling like his choices were the main thrust behind the resurgence of the cancer.

The next day came, and the phone rang early in the morning. It was Dr. Jurrida. Would more bad news be forthcoming? As Jason's father listened to the doctor on the phone, his countenance went from grim to gleeful as Dr. Jurrida explained that the MRI results had been wrongly interpreted. Because of an additional variable added into the tests that followed, they showed that the tumor, in fact, had not grown and that Jason was effectively in a state of remission! Relief and rejoicing inevitably followed.

The last few days had been excruciating, and perhaps, in the end, the Lord had heard their pleas to finish the miracle that they had witnessed over the last couple of years.

In the months that followed, Jason's condition continued to improve. Jason's dad made several entries into his journal during this time, although the entries became less frequent.

> March 12, 2003: Jason is still struggling with his cold and the medicine. Patty is not sure if he has just had enough or if the dose is a little high. I feel we should keep Jason on and Patty feels the Lord has healed him. I am suggesting the Lord is working through the medicine. This side of eternity we may not know.

> April 15, 2003: Tax Day. Dr. Jurrida called and received Jason's scans. Dr. Burzynski and he have decided to move Jason onto the pill form. This day is just another milestone in God's goodness to our family.

> April 22, 2003: We feel very blessed. We are heading to the Burzynski Clinic to have Jason go on the pill form and to come off the infusion pump. We met many people at the clinic, and we made every effort to encourage all that were there. We met with Mike Goldberg and Greg Burzynski regarding the publicity of Jason's case.

Jason would now consume seventy-two pills a day for the next several months as part of an ongoing antineoplaston treatment. The doctors insisted that the Merkle family stay the course to ensure the body's success in warding off any remaining cancer cells. It is a little bit like when you kill a wasp or a hornet that has invaded your home.

You don't just smack the wasp or hornet once with the swatter; you hit it multiple times to ensure that the pest is completely dead. Why risk hitting it only once and then face the possibility of its retaliating against you?

In essence, Jason had come full circle. Just less than two years earlier, he had been given a death sentence and told by doctors to go carry out a bucket list of things to do before he died. Yet, at that very moment, a twenty-year-old man responded with indignant repudiation to such an action. Instead, he and his family decided to fight death with a sword—and not just with any sword, but with the "sword of the Spirit." Ephesians 6:11–17 states,

> Put on the full armor of God so that you can take your stand against the devil's schemes. For our struggle is not against flesh and blood, but against the rulers, against the authorities, against the powers of this dark world and against the spiritual forces of evil in the heavenly realms. Therefore, put on the full armor of God, so that when the day of evil comes, you may be able to stand your ground, and after you have done everything, to stand. Stand firm then, with the belt of truth buckled around your waist, with the breastplate of righteousness in place, and with your feet fitted with readiness that comes from the gospel of peace. In addition to all this, take up the shield of faith, with which you can extinguish all the flaming arrows of the evil one. Take the helmet of salvation and the sword of the Spirit, which is the word of God.

Still the question remains, how exactly did Jason Merkle beat terminal brain cancer when all of the experts insisted he had no more than one year to live? The pragmatist might be quick to argue that the Burzynski Clinic provided a superior cancer alternative with which to fight one of the most deadly and puzzling diseases on the planet. On the other hand, the Christian would be quick to object to this notion, putting forth that God, himself, is the ultimate healer, and it was because of Jason's great faith that he overcame the disease. An agnostic or atheist may even assert that Jason's positive attitude and support, combined with savvy medical science, simply beat all the odds, proving that no fate is written in stone, but rather all humans have a choice on how to respond to difficult situations.

But recall one more time his brother's prayer in December 2001 in a call of desperation for Jason to be healed in exactly one year's time. There's no arguing the fact that, according to Jason, in one year's time precisely, the tumor completely disappeared. Now, some people would call this a staggering coincidence. However, it may just be the kind of miracle that proves that God hears the prayers of all people, and some of the world's most impactful prayers come from those still seeking to prove his existence. In this case, God turned Matthew's simultaneously doubtful and hopeful prayer into an inescapably beautiful display of his glory and majesty, healing the man no one said could be healed.

Of Jason's four brothers, Jordan may have struggled the most with Jason's diagnosis of cancer. According to Jason's mother, Jordan expressed to her on several occasions that Jason's condition nearly caused Jordan to completely turn his back on God. In Jordan's mind, the disease with which his brother was afflicted seemed to be unfair. How could God, who was called all-loving, allow Jason to combat such a nefarious, crippling disease? While Jordan was away at college as Jason was being treated, he wrestled with God and decided he would either be "all in" or "all out." In other words, he would give his life over to God and trust him no matter what the circumstance, or he would withdraw and live the life of a committed agnostic or atheist. In the end, Jordan chose to be all in for God. Here was yet another way that God used Jason's cancer to teach those around him about his purpose for their lives.

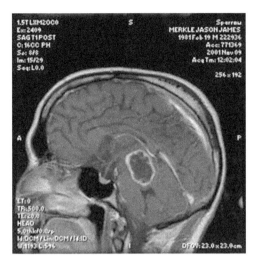

Shown here at the center of the brain,
the tumor is about the size of a golf ball.

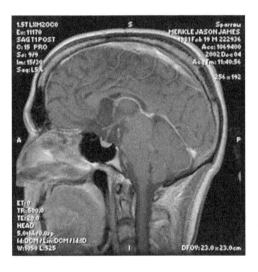

The tumor has completely disappeared just one year later.

*Setbacks may come. Stay focused. Fight the good fight. Finish the race.
Keep the faith.*

Chapter 18

New Life

After all the Merkle family had been through, the battle continued for Jason. Just two weeks after going off infusion treatment, he was anxious to resume athletic activity. Playing in a church softball game, Jason slid into second base and broke his left arm. This was a devastating moment—it seemed as if the hits just kept coming. He simply could not resume a normal life. However, Jason chose not to view it this way. Instead, he chastised himself for not being patient enough with the work of healing that God was indeed doing in his body. After all, it would take time for his muscles and bones to gain their strength back, and his body was not accustomed to vigorous physical activity.

As time progressed, Jason was able to regain normal physical activity, but he pursued his goals more steadily and with a patience bestowed upon him by the Lord. The voice inside Jason's head kept repeating the statement, "Trust me, Jason. Trust Me."

What's more, as Jason's vision for his life became clearer, so did his physical vision. Jason's optician said that Jason was the only patient he had ever seen go from legally blind to perfect twenty-twenty vision. It was just another one of the miracles in Jason's story.

In the fall of 2003, Jason returned to Cedarville to finish his college career. He was elected by the student body to be part of an elite group on campus called the Advisory 7, a group that would serve to lead other students in worship and ministry. Pastor Rohm mentored Jason in this position. During the course of his junior and senior years, Jason gave three sermons at the chapel service. It was evident that he had become an outstanding public speaker, and his ability to communicate messages about the Lord seemed to come naturally to him. Jason graduated from Cedarville in 2005 as probably one of the most unlikely graduates on stage. He was not even supposed to be alive, let alone graduating fewer than four years after his diagnosis. Yet, there he was, alive and well. Jason was practically a celebrity on campus at Cedarville when he returned. Everyone knew him because his case was broadcast daily throughout the community each day in a call to prayer.

Jason explains, "I was very fortunate to survive. Some people don't want to talk about cancer, but the Lord has given me the desire and ability to do it. It's a huge blessing." In the summer of 2003, after Jason was fully recovered, three churches in the Lansing area organized a choir sing-along praise service together and honored Jason with the opportunity to share his incredible story. It was just the beginning of how Jason would share his miracle with others in the years to come.

Even though Jason's tumor was no longer malignant, the benign form of the mass still remained due to calcification, which meant that he still had to contend with the shunt in his brain diverting fluid away from the skull in order for him to live a normal life. About five years after recovering from cancer and after he had begun his new life with his wife, Kristen, his shunt broke a second time. According to Jason, he knew it had happened because of the pressure he felt inside of his head. However, he had been through this before on a couple of occasions, and he decided to go about the business of his day as normal. He wanted to put off going to the hospital until after he had accomplished what he needed to do. Luckily for Jason, nothing happened before his arrival at the hospital that evening. Seeing it as more of a nuisance than a life-threatening circumstance, Jason will tell you that he made a bad decision in not going immediately to the hospital that day. Still, he had been through such a great deal already that a shunt breaking inside of his brain seemed like small potatoes compared to fighting the seemingly unbeatable foe of brain cancer.

Today, Jason is a husband and father of four. He shares his testimony with cancer patients and community members alike whenever he has an opportunity. In the years since Jason's remission, he has shared his story with multiple groups at schools, churches, and youth groups. In fact, this is how he met his wife, as she was in the audience during one of his testimonials.

Every week, Jason gets calls and e-mails from fellow cancer patients who want to inquire about his method of healing. His is such a remarkable story that rarely does a week go by without his sharing his incredible story of healing with someone in a similar condition facing an uphill battle. Jason's message from a practical standpoint is this: do the research, and take matters into your own hands; find survivors of your particular cancer and challenge doctors to also find survivors that they have treated; cut out the sugar, as cancer eats sugar ten to twelve times the rate of healthy cells according to BeatCancer. org; begin an alkaline diet consisting primarily of vegetables; and avoid chemo and radiation unless there is proven success for your particular cancer in terms of high percentage survival rates. The substantive part of his testimony is primarily that, in spite of our human doubtfulness, God has a plan for each and every person. When things get dark and gloomy and it seems like no light is in sight, it is in this place that the Lord teaches us to trust in him and him alone. Cancer is primarily conquered through heavy prayer and trusting in God alone to guide you along the path for healing. For Jason, that path was clearly the Burzynski Clinic.

Every year, Jason goes for an MRI to see if the tumor is, indeed, still in remission. Up until a year ago, the tumor was in a benign state and smaller than it was when they discovered it in 1994. In fact, it's morphed into a tiny, calcified cyst that is still large enough to prevent proper drainage of fluid in the brain, which is why the shunt remains in his head. However, fear of the mass rearing its ugly head again in the form of a malignancy has caused Jason to be unconventional in his actions as a way to be proactive against the causes of malignancies. For example, he often drinks baking soda mixed with water because baking soda is at the top of the alkaline food chain. Research shows that alkaline foods are cancer-fighting machines. Moreover, he rarely eats anything with large amounts of sugar and never drinks soda. He only drinks water on a consistent basis—it's all his body needs. It's actually all any of our bodies need, but we are inundated in American culture with sugar-rich drinks such as soda, lemonade, juices, and so on.

Not long ago, Jason had yet another MRI completed, and to save money he goes to specialized clinics to have them performed. The average cost at a clinic is four hundred to five hundred dollars versus twenty-five hundred dollars at local hospitals. It should be noted that each new MRI is compared with previous MRIs. When the last doctor reviewed Jason's scan, he made some peculiar notes that Jason noted in the margins: "Tumor seems to have shrunk since last MRI—radiation appears to be effective."

Of course, Jason has never received radiation, nor was he receiving anything of the kind in between subsequent MRIs. In fact, in the last year, he had increased his commitment to drinking his "baking soda shakes" once a day rather than just every once in a while. While the medical community may tell you that radiation or chemotherapy is the only way to shrink a tumor, Jason Merkle is living proof that this is a false conclusion. Jason's father elaborates: "God's hand was definitely on Jason's life, but one of the key reasons for Jason's survival was a change in diet. Three-cancer enhancing agents are high-acidity foods, sugar, and lack of oxygen. If the human body can reach a ketosis state, achieved by an all-alkaline diet, and add in exercise, thereby increasing oxygen levels in the body, these are cancer killers. Also, we did not eat meat with any secondary antibiotics injected, which is why the elk meat was such a blessing. And of course, the Burzynski Clinic was phenomenal. We may have not been able to shrink the tumor without it. It was a physical, spiritual, and psychological fight. We watched funny movies and laughed as often as we could in spite of the misery. It was a real fight for survival, but a 'joyful heart is good medicine'" (Prov. 17:22).

Today, Jason would tell you what his life and near death have taught him:

- Give each day to the Lord. Realize it is a gift he has given to you.
- Live every day like it might be your last. Spend time with your loved ones.
- Don't just leave a legacy. Live a legacy.
- Get out of your comfort zone; that is where you will grow the most. Help others.
- Stay active mentally, physically, and spiritually.
- Walk by faith, not by sight.
- Be intentional, pay attention to details, and be determined!
- Be generous. Be quick to forgive. Be a servant to others. Love unconditionally.
- Our time here is limited. Don't waste it.
- Smile and laugh as often as possible.

Live life to the fullest but not selfishly. Find every way you can to give your body the advantage to win the fight. Laugh and smile!

Chapter 19

The Burzynski Enigma

S ince 1977, Dr. Stanislaw Burzynski has been treating cancer patients with his alternative antineoplaston formula. And since the beginning, he has been fighting a war with both the FDA and the Texas State Medical Board to keep his medical license. Despite the proven effectiveness of antineoplastons on many cancer patients, including saving the lives of many people who were written off with no hope for survival by traditional oncologists, Burzynski's cutting-edge treatment has agitated pharmaceutical companies that are profiting from chemotherapy and radiation technology. In the case that lasted nearly ten years between the Texas State Medical Board and the Burzynski Clinic, the board admitted that "the efficacy of antineoplastons in the treatment of human cancers is not of issue in these proceedings." This is a shocking statement since it would seem that the most important criteria for licensing of a medical clinic would be the efficacy of treatment, considering that the improved health of the patients and the eradication of cancer should be the primary objectives. Beneath the cryptic position of both the Texas State Medical Board and large cancer centers such as MD Anderson is the fear that, ultimately, Burzynski's methodology will replace a multibillion-dollar industry that relies on chemotherapy and radiation alone to treat cancer patients. Of course, the primary difference between Burzynski's innovative therapy and the one ordained by the FDA is that antineoplastons do not attack healthy cells—only cancer cells—whereas chemotherapy and radiation target healthy cells as well. Chemotherapy patients often end up in a neutropenic state, with precariously low white blood cell counts, and radiation patients often never recover in the specific areas that the radiation targeted.

Ultimately, the Texas State Medical Board lost the battle with Burzynski in 1996, but they renewed their battle in 2012, going after the clinic this time for prescribing gene-targeted cancer regimens in conjunction with antineoplastons (phenylbutyrate). In essence, Burzynski takes a blood sample and a tissue sample to determine which prescription medication best fits individual cancer patients and administers those drugs along with his antineoplaston regimen. This has proven effective in multiple patients, as Dr. Erik R. Carlson, professor and residency director at the University of Tennessee, attests: "Dr. Burzynski is out of the box, and that is what Ms. Wright (Carlson's cancer patient) needed. She needed fresh ideas. This stuff is not taught to you in medical school. The curriculum is very vanilla." In essence, Burzynski is using what is called personalized gene-targeted cancer therapy to fight the cancer. Richard A. Jaffe, Burzynski's attorney, said, "When the cancer establishment out there tells you are going to die, you have to die. But why should a chemotherapist tell you this?" In short, they are the experts, and if the patients live in spite of their best expertise and their best knowledge, then they are no longer experts at all. They are discredited and put out of business.

According to www.cancer.gov, antineoplastons have rendered undeniable success. The website states the following history:

> Antineoplaston A was further purified and yielded antineoplastons A1, A2, A3, A4, and A5. These mixtures of seven to thirteen peptides were patented in 1985. In vitro tissue culture studies and in vivo toxicity studies in animal models were performed for antineoplastons A1 through A5. According to the

developer, each individual fraction had a higher level of antitumor activity and lower toxicity level than antineoplaston A. Phase I trials of this antineoplaston group in patients with various advanced cancers showed A2 as contributing to the highest tumor response rate, so it was selected for further study.

In layman's terms, this means that early studies indicated that antineoplaston 2 was proving effective. The website goes on to say,

Although several possible mechanisms of action and theories about the activity of antineoplastons have been proposed, specifically for antineoplaston A10, none of the theories has been conclusively demonstrated. One theoretical mechanism of action proposes that antineoplaston A10 is specifically capable of intercalating with DNA at specific base pairs and thereby might interfere with carcinogens binding to the DNA helix. This interweaving of A10 into the DNA helix may be capable of interfering with DNA replication, transcription, or translation. The theory is based on the manipulation of molecular models of DNA and A10; however, no published evidence of the creation of this actual molecule or evidence of the properties ascribed to it exists in the medical literature.

Essentially, A10 has proven effective in the eradication of cancer cells, and the clinic admits that they can only theorize about how the antineoplaston works since by and large the medical world is not interested in the technology. More than likely, antineoplastons have remained an FDA trial for so long because of one of two reasons: one, time and resources are not being spent on the innovation; or two, the results would effectively upend the current model for cancer treatment, thus costing the drug companies and cancer centers billions of dollars.

Jason's story, like seventy-two others, is posted on the Burzynski website for others to read. When Jason's parents asked his neurosurgeon what he would do if it was his child who had been diagnosed with brain cancer, the surgeon indicated that he would probably forego the chemotherapy and radiation treatment and just let Jason die. Since chemo and radiation would only harm Jason's body and ultimately offered no hope for survival, the neurosurgeon issued a hopeless verdict to the Merkles. In fact, according to www.cureyourowncancer.org, nine out of ten oncologists would reject chemotherapy or radiation in treating their own cancer. It is because of statistics like these that Jason and his family believe that the negative effects of chemotherapy and radiation kill more people than cancer itself.

Without a question, cancer, in all its forms, is a devastating disease that affects children, middle-aged people, and the elderly alike, and it is appalling that alternative cancer treatment centers like the Burzynski Clinic, who have demonstrated proven success, are frowned upon by the oncology world. It can be argued that many oncologists are trained to simply perform the treatments that have been tested and approved by the FDA, and since they have all been indoctrinated with an identical method of treatment, they simply scoff at anything beyond the scope of mainstream medicine. However, cancer research is showing now that targeted gene therapy can be very effective in treating each patient as an individual, rather than as a lab rat.

As already stated, antineoplastons have saved many lives that were written off by the oncological experts. Jason recounts several people having success at the Burzynski Clinic—both patients who were with him at the clinic when he was staying there and patients who chose to go the clinic in the years that followed. Unfortunately, as Jason admits, many patients who experience initial success are unable to finish the race. More than a few Burzynski patients who Jason knew personally lost the battle to cancer after going off treatment. Almost all of these patients had experienced the euphoria of seeing their cancer dissipate, but they were unwilling or unable to stay on the treatment for the recommended period of time. As in Jason's own story, even after almost two years of infusion treatment, he had to continue on the pill form of the antineoplastons for several months. Jason explains, "Most of the time there is no easy, wide-open road to beating cancer. Some people want quick and easy cures, and I don't blame them for that, but in my experience, it's a long, hard road that leads to success."

While at the funerals of people who have lost their battles with cancer, Jason has noticed that feelings of tragedy and disappointment are palpable. "People change course and fail because of a flawed strategy in life. Not quitting is not just about willpower because we all have moments of weakness, but it's about overcoming feelings of terror and helplessness by fueling one's self on the power of an everlasting and providential Father." Indeed, cancer survivors usually have one thing in common—they are compulsively optimistic in spite of the circumstances.

Jason also noticed that many people who were at the Burzynski Clinic did not supplement their treatment with a healthy diet. "Some people I knew there even went to the Cheesecake Factory every day to eat." There is a propensity for human beings to be resistant to change, even change that might save their lives. Jason would contend that most Americans are addicted to sugar and carbs. Like all things in life, carbohydrates and sugar can be enjoyed in moderation when a person is cancer free. But if a person truly wants to win the fight against cancer, he or she must often take drastic measures to defeat the enemy within. These measures may sound crazy and unconventional to the medical world, but God is not limited by medicine; he is only limited by people's lack of faith and determination. Jay Merkle sums it up this way:

> I am reminded of the book of Daniel in the Bible, specifically Daniel 1:8 where Daniel determines not to defile himself with King Nebuchadnezzar's food. Daniel steps out in faith, choosing to eat choice

vegetables and drink only water. And in Daniel 1:9, God blesses Daniel with favor and compassion because of his act of faith. Many people cannot discipline themselves, choosing short-term pleasure in eating what they want that, in essence, shorten their days. Of course, God could choose to heal any of us just by touching our bodies when we are sick, but often he calls on us to be proactive in faith. I can only imagine what doctors are going to look at fifty years from now as relates to radiation and chemo. They are going to find out they were doing everything wrong. In short, the body has the ability to fight cancer, but we have to give it the proper ammunition to conquer the enemy within.

Put another way, not quitting is one of the greatest challenges in battling cancer. Immediate success can often be a curse for people fighting any kind of malignancy because cancer, like a mole in the ground, can disappear and then suddenly pop up again unexpectedly. Eating the right foods and getting on a treatment like the Burzynski Clinic's antineoplaston regimen is essential, but staying on that path for the long haul is where ultimate victory can be achieved.

In sum, conventional doctors will often give patients a prospective amount of time to live when they are diagnosed with cancer. These educated guesses are based upon records of other patients who had varying life spans in the losing battle against particular cancers. In fact, many doctors do not refer to death as a lost battle, but rather refer to how they prolonged these patients' lives by a certain amount of time through chemotherapy or radiation. Some doctors will acknowledge that chemotherapy and radiation will extend the lives of patients but will in fact lower the quality of their lives while not eliminating the cancer. In essence, while it is not always the case that radiation and chemotherapy are ineffective against cancer, it is always the case that chemotherapy and radiation will temporarily or permanently harm the patient. More importantly. though, in cases where the patient's situation is dire (i.e., the patient is labeled terminal or is in the late stages), chemotherapy and radiation are only used to extend the patient's life (even if the quality of life is quite poor), not cure the disease. Jason believes that terminal patients may live longer by improving their diets and changing their lifestyles instead of being treated with chemotherapy or radiation.

Jason has seen multiple friends die of cancer, even after being treated with chemotherapy and radiation. Some have even had surgical procedures to remove all or part of the cancer. It is a heartbreaking process, indeed, to watch a patient decline from the effects of cancer on the body. The body is not designed to endure toxic treatments like chemotherapy or radiation, which is why these kinds of things would never be given to healthy people. Instead, there are plenty of natural ways to fight cancer using the nutrients that God has provided in the world.

During the nineteenth century, bloodletting was considering a cutting-edge approach to fighting disease, employing the theory that eliminating the diseased blood from the patient's body could eliminate the disease over time. Today, this practice is outlawed and considered to be an absurdity, as the medical community knows that this is entirely the wrong approach to fighting disease, with the exception of a few, rare cases. Jason believes through his research and multiple other sources that, not long from now, the medical community will consider chemotherapy and radiation to be far too toxic to be used as an option for cancer patients. The fact is that chemotherapy and radiation treatments are administered to patients in the hope that that the drugs and radiation will kill the cancer before they kill the patient.

Chemotherapy and radiation are highly effective against some cancers, as Jason would admit. Even though these treatments may be toxic, they can be successful. Often the condition and health of the patients can improve their own chances. In the right circumstances, with faith, family, and friends, anything is possible.

Alternative treatments, like the kind of plan offered by the Burzynski Clinic, are becoming and more and more prevalent, and people should do their research on all the options before choosing the best path. In short, the Burzynski treatment, paired with a diet change, can be challenging for many people. The diet change alone can the biggest barrier for any patient. Even the prospect of death itself is not enough to encourage many people to make new lifestyle choices. However, Jason is living proof that diet choices can have a huge effect in one's battle with cancer—it is an undeniable fact that sugar is a cancer enhancer, and alkaline foods, such as broccoli and many other vegetables, are cancer inhibitors. Many doctors in the medical community will not acknowledge this for one reason or another, but the proof of the pudding is in the eating. Every person must do the research.

The question remains of how people can see so much early success with alternative treatments only to change their course and go back to conventional treatments. The pressure from the medical community will be extremely high, and all people want to believe that doctors always have each patient's best interests in mind. But remember this: people like Jason believe that the cancer survival rate should be much higher than the medical community lets on. A multibillion-dollar enterprise is not going to kowtow to a revolutionary approach to cancer that will bankrupt the industry. In the end, lasting, irreversible transformation comes from the Lord and the Lord alone; everything outside of God's providence is bound to fail. So if it is a person's time to die, it's his or her time to die; God's will is always to heal us, whether in this life or the next.

Find the best possible resources and utilize them. Look for proof of success. Be willing to think outside the box.

Chapter 20

Return to Africa

While on a high school mission trip in 1997, Jason felt the call of the Lord to go to Africa and serve there. As previously stated, Jason was perplexed by this notion since he did not have the slightest desire to serve there and it seemed absurd to travel so far away to a culture so foreign to him. Jason wrestled with God on this for several years, purposely postponing and circumventing plans to go.

In God's own way, he used Jason's illness to introduce him to the great continent of Africa, securing for him and his family a safari trip with all expenses paid by two separate hunting outfits in South Africa.

What Jason didn't know at the time was that this hunting trip during his battle with brain cancer would not be his only visit. God would call him to go again, but next time he would call him in a larger capacity to serve a greater need at a time when his health was fully restored. In the summer of 2017, Pastor Jeff approached Jason about ministry needs in Nigeria, which of course is located on the continent of Africa. Pastor Jeff is one of the founders of Back-to-Back ministries. Back-to-Back is a nonprofit Christian organization with a vision to serve and support orphans, impoverished children, and widows throughout the world. This organization looks to uplift disadvantaged children by providing them with the tools to become mature, Christian adults and break the cycle of generational poverty. Helping these kids to know Jesus Christ as their Lord and Savior is the crux of their mission.

At thirty-six years of age, fifteen years removed from his battle with the brain tumor, Jason traveled to Nigeria to work in the orphanages and help the staff and locals develop better farming skills to support the staff and children at these orphanages. Despite Back-to-Back's presence at these orphanages in Nigeria, the food supply is mitigated by poor farming techniques, lack of government resources, and lack of education. Children at these orphanages often only eat one meal a day—a large bowl of rice, chicken, and carrots (if available) at around four or five o' clock in the afternoon, when they get home from school. This means no breakfast and no lunch, which means many of these children are malnourished and starving by the time they get home from school.

Jason admitted that, despite the inherent need of the destitute in Nigeria, he was nervous about the trip. He could feel himself wrestling with the Lord again considering the possibility of leaving his wife and children behind. "I did not want Kristen to know this, but terrorist attacks happen in Nigeria, especially the northern part where there is a heavy Muslim presence." Just before Jason's trip, there was an attack just outside of Nigeria that killed four or five Americans. But Jason's trust in the Lord superseded his fears of death. Before he left, he explained to Kristen the particulars of their financial situation, which he normally handled, in case something happened to him. "Cast your cares upon the Lord, and he will sustain you. He will never let the righteous fall" (Ps. 55:22). Jason would not let his fears and worries deter him. After all, the Lord had always called him to go to Africa, and this time, he would have the opportunity to serve others.

Jason traveled with Pastor Jeff and Jonathan, director of operations for Back-to-Back Ministries in Nigeria, and another missionary whose name was Clay. They flew into the city of Abuja in the Federal

Capital Territory. When Jason arrived, he could tell immediately he was in an impoverished country. Much of the airport was without electrical power, and it was noticeably dirty and unkempt. After retrieving their luggage, they were immediately greeted by street peddlers of all kinds, selling sugarcane, nuts of all kinds, and many other items. Of course, none of the foods were safe to eat, and so Jason was advised to not buy anything.

Daniel and Fred, two men associated with Back-to-Back Ministries, picked the men up in a van and drove out of the airport. Daniel explained to Jason that the road going out of the airport was the most well-maintained road in all of Nigeria. Many of the roads throughout the country were in disrepair. What's more, the interstates were chaotic. Despite overpasses being built for pedestrians, people and animals were constantly crossing the road at will, jamming up traffic and causing mayhem. There simply was no order. Markets of all kinds lined the roads, petitioning travelers to stop and purchase their handmade items, foods, and so on. Because of this, traffic could be backed up for miles if cars slowed or stopped and blocked traffic. Daniel and Fred stopped the van at one of these markets so that the men could buy water and other prepackaged foods for the trip ahead. Jason bought a Snickers bar and water.

An hour or so later, Jason and the team arrived at a four-star hotel and resort where they would eat dinner. This was one of the only safe places for Westerners to eat. It was also inexpensive from an American's point of view, as one dollar was equivalent to three hundred and fifty naira (the Nigerian currency). After eating, Jason and the team traveled to a Catholic convent to spend the night. The place was guarded by a heavy, metal, opaque gate. Jason and his team were told not to drink the water and to brush their teeth with bottled water. It was pitch black with little lighting in the building, except the guests had power in their small bedrooms. According to Jason, it was extremely hot inside his room as there was no air conditioning. Luckily, there was an overhead fan, which he turned on before he went to sleep. At two in the morning, he woke up in a sweat because the power had gone out, leaving the overhead fan nonoperational.

He opened up his window and suddenly heard a bunch of guys yelling and screaming and playing music out in the streets. Due to the extreme heat and noise, Jason did not sleep much this first night.

The next day, the missionary team set out for their destination. which was the city of Jos, boasting a population of nine hundred thousand. Jos is in the plateau state that received six months of rain a year, followed by six months of complete dryness. The five- to six-hour drive was bumpy and long. Because Jason was in the middle seat in the van, he became very sick to his stomach. The band of travelers had to stop, and Jeff offered to give the front seat to Jason to help with his motion sickness. Fred, one of the drivers, gave Jason some medicine for the motion sickness—it was a common occurrence on Nigerian roads.

The next day, Jason was exhausted and drained, but the trip continued regardless. Over the next week, Jason and the team visited five orphanages. Pastor Jeff and Jonathan brought with them several letters from the United States for children at the orphanages who were being sponsored by American families. Jason noticed immediately how well behaved and grateful the children were for their presents and encouragement. "Their faces lit up when we read the letters out loud to the kids. It made their day, their week, and their month." After reading the letters, Pastor Jeff taught a Bible lesson, and the kids were quiet and attentive throughout. These kids had such contentment and joy because they were being taken care of when so many were not.

Because many of the caretakers at the orphanages are women, there is a desperate need for male presence in the lives of these children. Many of the boys would hold Jason's hand and listen intently when he spoke, desperate for male attention. "Lack of male leadership is evident," Jason explained. "Many of the women are willing to work, but many of the men abuse their time with other things." Some of these orphans were abandoned altogether, some of their families had died, and still others were left by their parents because they could not afford to feed and provide for them. Sometimes, a few of these orphans would visit their families on the weekends, but these were the fortunate ones.

In addition, it did not take Jason long to discover that much of Nigeria was lacking even an elementary education. In fact, Jason had overheard talk that one of the governors in a nearby state of Nigeria had recently tested forty thousand high school teachers, and twenty thousand had failed a fourth-grade test. This was a classic example of the blind leading the blind.

The Lord reminded Jason on this mission trip that his plight with a brain tumor was grave, indeed, but these Nigerian people and children face dire circumstances day in and day out, fighting for survival much like he had on a daily basis just fifteen years prior. In this way, God used Jason's cancer to equip him not only to feel pity for these suffering people but more importantly to exhibit the love that God has for them in his commitment to teach them better farming techniques and to spend quality time with them. Jason Munafo, the director of Back-to-Back in Nigeria, explained that people often died very young of treatable diseases, such as malaria, heart conditions, or strokes. He indicated that he had attended an inordinate number of funerals in Nigeria as compared with back home in the States. Access to quality health care was lacking.

While Jason's days there were full, his belly was not. Most of the time, he ate cans of tuna fish to avoid ingesting any kind of food-borne illness. He worked many of the days on the seventy-five-acre farm teaching the Nigerians how to better care for their plants—for example, they did not know how to stake their tomato plants to allow for optimal growth. In addition, Jason showed them techniques for properly raising and caring for chickens. Many of the chickens that were raised were sold to a restaurant called Mr. Biggs to help support the staff and children at the orphanages. Because Jason had raised his own chickens in the United States, he taught them how to care for chickens in the proper way. As Jason and the team were driving in Nigeria, Jason also noted that the cattle he saw driving down the roads looked to be anorexic compared to cattle in the States, with little fat to cover the bones protruding through their skin. Simply put, the cattle did not have enough to eat because the farmers who raised them were not educated on how to properly provide for their needs, not to mention the lack of resources available to them.

On one particular day, Jason and his team visited a widows' market in which several women were selling items to support themselves and their children. "I was blown away by it. We entered into the area, and there were about thirty women who broke out in song for us. They welcomed us with their music, and then we purchased some of their goods. All of these products were handmade, such as wallets, purses, and dresses."

As Jason's time in Nigeria came to an end on the trip, he reflected on his two weeks in a world that seemed broken and poor to the outside world. "The Nigerian people won my heart over," he said. "They were completely accepting, loving, and eager to receive help from missionaries. They were not stubborn or arrogant. They were happy despite their poverty." Jason added that the people—in particular, the women—seemed willing to work hard to provide for their families. Matthew 5:3–6 states, "Blessed are the poor in spirit, for theirs is the kingdom of heaven. Blessed are those who mourn, for they shall be comforted. Blessed are the meek for they shall inherit the earth. Blessed are those who hunger and thirst for righteousness, for they shall be satisfied." The Nigerian people were, indeed, blessed, in ways that are hard for Westerners to contemplate or describe.

On the way back to Abuja from Jos, Fred and Jason talked a long while about what it takes to be successful in a country like Nigeria, and Fred indicated that one had to own a business in order to excel. One thing Jason noticed is that, while there was an abundance of chicken restaurants, there were no coffee shops—an astute observation coming from a man who does not drink coffee. Fred agreed that, while Nigerians like coffee, this was missing from their culture. So Fred and Jason began drafting a business plan to start a coffee shop. When Jason got back to the States, Fred called him a couple of times a week to continue working on their vision for the shop. Both were excited about this opportunity. One day, Jason received a call from the director of Back-to-Back saying that Fred had died suddenly of a stroke while making another run to and from the airport. Fred left behind a wife and children. Jason, devastated by the news, recalled Jason Munafo's comments about short life spans and lack of medical care in Nigeria. Fred, too, was a victim of the poor care, as his life may have been saved if he had gotten proper treatment in time.

The vision for the coffee shop, however, has not died. Jason intends to go back to Nigeria and carry out the plan that he and Fred had set their minds to in late 2017. One of the visions Fred had was to print Bible verses on all the cups of coffee they served so that people who purchased coffee at the new shop could quench their thirst for the Lord while having a small cup of joe.

Be content. Serve others. Giving is an opportunity, not just a donation. Giving is sometimes best in the form of service.

Epilogue

In July 2001, Jason Merkle was told by his doctor that he was about to receive the worst news he was ever going to hear. He then proceeded to tell Jason that he had a tumor at the bottom of his brain stem that was most definitely fatal—he had as little as two months to live or at most a year with chemotherapy and radiation treatment. The quality of Jason's life would diminish quickly from this point forward, and he had better be sure to do all the things he ever wanted to do in the short time he had left.

Yet this news turned out not to be the worst news Jason was ever going to hear for two important reasons. The first reason is obvious: Jason miraculously survived this fatal tumor and became conditioned to live a life fully committed to God, relying solely upon him for provision and protection. He beat all the insurmountable odds and now has a story to share that has impacted hundreds, if not thousands, of cancer patients throughout the United States. His is a story of great hope to many people, and while that is seemingly the most important reason that having deadly brain cancer was not the worst news he would ever hear, there is a more important reason.

The worst news that someone can ever hear is not that they have a deadly disease and only a few months to live. The absolute worst news one can ever hear is that God's face has turned against him or her—that his or her soul is in danger of hell. Matthew 10:28 states, "Do not be afraid of those who kill the body but cannot kill the soul. Rather, be afraid of the One who can destroy both soul and body in hell." In short, the death of the body is of no great consequence if the fate of the soul is secure through faith in Jesus Christ.

Conclusion

Written by Jason Merkle

I often sit and watch my children play, and I stop to think about how blessed I am to have them. If the Lord had not saved me from brain cancer, I would not be here, and neither would they. I would not have met my wonderful wife, Kristen, and I would have missed out on so many other wonderful experiences. I have a great deal to live for, and I am grateful for the time given to me.

Life's trials often drive people in one of two directions. Out of suffering and pain can come great joy and a desire to fight the good fight, or resentment and bitterness sew a seed of fear, thus destroying one's potential. My hope is that each person who reads this book will choose a life of joy despite his or her circumstances. It is not the circumstance that dictates one's fate; rather it is one's attitude that determines one's success or failure.

Truly, to have gone through all these tribulations without faith, family, and friends would have been impossible. Each person should latch onto faith, family, and friends during challenging times just as much as in the good times. Every day, I continually work to keep my body healthy. My approach to life is to give my body the best chance at preventing disease instead of just waiting to get sick again. I continue to drink my green drinks (see below) and water. Water is the only liquid our bodies really need! Moreover, I limit my sugar and flour intake, and I keep my body active. A body in motion stays in motion, but a body at rest may find its final, earthly rest sooner rather than later.

I have witnessed many people who retire become ill within just a few months or few years of their retirement. Their lifestyle begins to resemble that of someone in a vegetative state, as they sit around and do nothing for hours on end. Our bodies are meant to keep working and keep playing! Since the opening chapters in the Bible, Adam and Eve were created to work in the garden. We never should really retire until it is actually time to retire from this earth. Everyone should stay active and work to eat right. We choose what our bodies are made out of each day by what we choose to eat. "You are what you eat" is a true cliché, indeed, but the truth is even deeper than that. We should never get too comfortable in life because comfort is the enemy of progress. People should be invigorated by the days of their lives, taking on new challenges, working hard, playing hard, and doing their best to be healthy individuals. DOn't quIT growing, and never settle for the status quo!

During the worst moments of my fight against cancer, I looked and felt terrible. I often got strange looks from people, and their comments were not always kind. We should all treat people the way we want to be treated, regardless of the circumstances. Jesus states in Matthew 22:37, "You shall love the Lord your God with all your heart and with all your soul and with all your mind. This is the greatest commandment. And a second is like it: You shall love your neighbor as yourself." All of us have a very limited time on Earth, and we need to love one another, encourage good behaviors, and help others in need. To do these things is to build treasures in heaven and not on earth. Following Jesus' greatest commandment is to live with an eternal perspective—we come into this life with nothing, and we will undoubtedly leave with nothing. My advice is to take time each day to help others. If we live each day caring more about others, we will have greater contentment ourselves.

Last, take time to pray and discern what God's plan is for your life. And once you find it (and find it you will!), pursue it with all your heart. Proverbs 16:9 states, "The heart of man plans his way, but the Lord establishes his steps."

In closing, there are so many people I would like to thank. So many of you out there helped, prayed, and encouraged me as I traveled this long and winding road. The road was much less treacherous with you all by my side! I wish I could put every single person's name in this book, but there's no way for me to do that as the list may be longer than this entire book itself. The Lord has been good to me, and I am blessed by each one of you who took the time and effort to care for me during my most challenging days. The Lord is good no matter what, despite the circumstances and despite the outcome.

Most of all, I am grateful for my parents. They were the main driving force in keeping me in a mind-set of never quitting. When things got bad, they were always there to pick me up. Moreover, they made prayerful decisions and worked tirelessly to always determine the best course of action. There was quite literally never any rest for them, but in spite of being exhausted themselves, they worked around the clock for me to give me the best opportunity to survive, especially in the first seven months of my battle, which were by far the most critical and challenging. They exhibited true, unconditional love for me as they pushed me and encouraged me to do more, try harder, and keep fighting. There is no how-to manual on dealing with a son who has terminal brain cancer, but fortunately, there is a how-to manual on prayer and the pursuit of God. My parents were shining examples of biblical people as they sacrificed all of themselves out of love for me, and they demonstrated a resilient faith in God that helped me to become a better man and a better follower of Christ.

We serve a wonderful, loving, and gracious God who never leaves or forsakes us. He has a plan, and that means there is a reason for everything that happens. Even when it looks like evil has prevailed, watch for how God will redeem the situation. He always does, each and every time. Finally, we need to live by faith, which is the assurance of things hoped for and the conviction of things not seen.

Back (Left to Right): Matt, Jason, Jonathan, Dan, Jordan
Front: Patty and Jay Merkle

DOn't quIT! Put on the full armor of God and fight.

Winning Strategy:

1. Most importantly, pray and believe in a higher power to heal you. (I choose Jesus Christ as my Lord and Savior).
2. Change your diet. Eliminate sugar, flour, dairy, and artificial sweeteners from your diet.
3. Drink only reverse-osmosis filtered water. Try to consume at least one gallon of water each day.
4. Seek professional help—research like crazy to find the best possible solution for treating your cancer. Find a treatment with as few possible side effects as possible. Find living proof of whatever treatments you find. The website www. chrisbeatcancer.com is a great place to start.
5. Turn your body alkaline to fight the cancer. Baking soda is a great way—one teaspoon in a glass of reverse-osmosis water every four hours.
6. Take vitamin supplements. Vitamin D deficiency is a very common factor in a lot of cancer patients. Seek out a nutritionist. Mine was Dr. Van Merkle: www.sciencebasednutrition.com
7. Make a green drink every day. Blend together a mixture of kale, spinach, chard, carrots, apple or banana, golden flax seeds, and raw eggs. Blend in a Vitamix blender for best results. (You could use many other healthy vegetables as well.)
8. Take a teaspoon of organic, raw, unfiltered, unpasteurized apple cider vinegar with the mother (live bacteria) with a glass of water twice a day.
9. Eat ginger and turmeric—both are cancer-fighting agents
10. Stay optimistic. A cheerful heart is good medicine. Never plan your funeral. Plan your future to live a long healthy life!

Questions to Ask Each Doctor

1. What do you recommend for treatments?
2. What are the side effects of your treatment(s)—both short term and long term?
3. How many survivors do you have with the treatment you just recommended for me?
4. What would you do if I were your child? (Some doctors told me that they would not treat me at all because they knew the trauma chemotherapy would cause.)
5. Are there other cancer clinics you recommend I talk with?
6. Are there any alternative options I should consider? Dr. Burzynski?

    www.cancermed.com; www.burzynskipatientgroup.org
7. Ask your doctor for living proof before doing anything.

A Recollection of Hairy Cell Leukemia

I t was September 2015. I had just left the medical center, where the nurse had drawn blood for my physical examination coming up in two weeks. My wife, Catherine, insisted that I get a physical, reasoning that our first child was due to be born in just seven months, and she thought it would be a good idea to check up on my overall health. I resisted at first, but there was no point in doing so. She insisted that I do it, and knowing that my resistance would be futile, I agreed.

I hated doctors. It's not that doctors are bad people or anything; it's just in all my life I had not received great news from doctors. While I never had any life-threatening illnesses, I had been plagued growing up with chronic ear infections—maladies that had led to two reconstructive ear surgeries, one at age fourteen and one while I was in college. In both instances, I had a cyst corroding my eardrum, and in order to remove the cyst on both occasions, the doctors had to remove a small portion of my eardrum, reconstructing the tissue both times using cartilage from the inside of my nose. While the surgeries both went according to plan, I had suffered terrible ear pain for much of my childhood. Often, I could not swim with the other kids in our backyard pool because of infections or pain. And it was more than just the ear problems. Whenever I went to a doctor, my blood pressure shot through the roof. At times, the nurses looked at me with frightened looks on their faces, wondering if they were about to watch a child have a heart attack. This went hand in hand with the generalized anxiety that I inherited from my mother. I had a great deal of anxiety about social situations and my own image, and so I spent some time on anxiety medication.

Not that any of the aforementioned problems were so terrible that they could not be overcome. I was lucky in many ways, and I knew, of course, that many people had it much worse. Still, doctors made me cringe, and I couldn't imagine that this time would be any different. This doctor, however, had one of the best demeanors I have ever been around. He helped me relax, he was easy to talk to, and he had a great bedside manner. So if I was going to have a physical, this was the man to do it with, no question.

After giving blood that day, I made my way to work. I worked in a sales position for a construction company, and it was one of the best positions I have ever held, and I had had many jobs up to this point in my life. I had just turned thirty-four the previous March, and I had worked a dozen other jobs since I was fifteen years old. On this particular day, I did not have as many sales calls scheduled because of my lab appointment and some other miscellaneous duties I wanted to get done at our home. I arrived home around two in the afternoon, and my wife was still at work. Suddenly, the phone rang, and I picked it up thinking it was one of my customers calling with a question about their order. When I picked it up, it was the nurse in Dr. Lundberg's office, my family physician. "Yes, Kyle, Dr. Lundberg wanted me to call you and tell you that we received your blood work today, and he said that you need to get to the emergency room immediately."

"What? What are you talking about? Why do I need to do that?" I asked, perplexed and dumbfounded. She repeated what she said before, and I asked to speak to the doctor.

Dr. Lundberg picked up the receiver and reiterated what the nurse had just told me. "Kyle, your platelets in your body are dangerously low—so low that you could even have a brain hemorrhage if they keep dropping."

I responded in disbelief. "I am sorry—what is happening here? I feel just fine."

And then Dr. Lundberg became irritated. "Kyle, I am telling you as your doctor that you need to go to the emergency room right now. Your blood work is showing dangerously low levels, and you need to just listen to me."

"Okay, okay. I am sorry," I replied. "I am just a little bit shocked." I hung up the phone and called my wife, and she drove straight home to take me to the emergency room. Although I am sure she was appalled by this development as well, she remained calm and tried to reassure me that all would be okay. We spent four to five hours in the emergency room that night as they performed another blood draw and took some X-rays and CT scans. They discovered that my spleen was severely enlarged and that my platelet count was indeed incredibly low. Platelets are the entities in the blood that are responsible for clotting functionality to prevent bleeding to death. Without platelets, people would bleed to death internally, or externally any time they got cut or had an abrasion.

The emergency room doctor surmised that I had a condition called idiopathic thrombocytopenic purpura (ITP), which can lead to excessive bleeding or bruising. However, he speculated that there was a chance, as well, that it could be a malignancy, but that was not his first suspicion. He would refer me to a blood specialist/oncologist who could do further research as to which condition was driving my platelets so low. Whereas normal people had anywhere from 140,000 to 250,000 platelets, I had a mere 40,000.

So I made an appointment with an blood specialist/oncologist the following week, and I was released from the hospital. While we were somewhat relieved to know that my life was not in immediate danger, both Catherine and I were anxious to find out what was causing this disorder and how to treat it.

In the previous months, I had been discovering bruises on my arms and legs, and before that time in my life, I had never bruised easily at all. So at this point, it seemed likely that I had this ITP condition and would have to spend the rest of my life on some medication. When we arrived at the oncologist's office that day, we were cautiously optimistic. Dr. Escobar walked into the room, sat down, and proceeded to immediately tell us his prediagnosis. "Based on your test results, I think this is some type of malignancy—either leukemia or lymphoma. We're not sure yet. We do not think it is ITP because the size of your spleen is about ten times the size of a normal spleen."

At this point, Catherine and I were winded. *Cancer? How could this be? How can we find out for sure?* Dr. Escobar explained that the only way to find out exactly what we were dealing with was to have a PET scan and also perform a bone-marrow biopsy. These two tests should indicate conclusively what kind of cancer I had and how to treat it. Dr. Escobar was ready to dismiss us, but my wife insisted that the biopsy be performed the same day. Dr. Escobar explained that was not how they do things and said I needed to schedule an appointment; however, Catherine was not taking no for an answer.

Dr. Escobar, friendly and accommodating as he would prove to be over the next few months, agreed but said, "It is going to be quite painful. Are you sure you want to do this today, Kyle?" I nodded reluctantly, as I felt my wife pushing me along.

The biopsy was indeed painful, even though they numbed the area at the top of the buttocks to perform the procedure. The nurse practitioner had a great deal of difficulty pulling the sample from my bone, so Dr. Escobar eventually had to extract the sample. I was glad when it was over, to say the least. Dr. Escobar said it would be two weeks before we got any results but that, in the meantime, we should schedule the PET scan at the hospital and then reconvene after both results were received.

Knowing people in the right places often comes in handy, and in this case, Catherine's cousin was the head of the radiology department at the hospital. She called us with the results of the PET scan, and the news was promising. There was no cancer detected in my liver or spleen; needless to say, we were encouraged by the news.

Because we were not supposed to be privileged to receive these results ahead of time, we waited for the doctor to call me or for my follow-up appointment—whichever came first. Two days later, I got the call. I was driving in my truck down a country road, having just left my last sales appointment and heading to the next. I answered, and Dr. Escobar said, "Hello, Kyle." I was a little taken aback, having not expected to receive a call from him personally. Usually the staff would call, or sometimes the nurse in these situations. I usually can read people fairly well, and Dr. Escobar's voice seemed low and subdued. "Kyle, I have received the results from your PET scan and from the biopsy, and while the good news is that the PET scan came back negative, your biopsy revealed that you are leukemic. It's a rare disorder called hairy cell leukemia. I am sorry to share this news with you, but—"

I interrupted. "So it's cancer?"

"Yes, I am afraid it is a malignancy that affects the white blood cells and the platelets, and this is what has caused the enlargement of your spleen."

I was nearly speechless, but I managed to ask, "How did I get this disease?"

"Unfortunately, we do not know the cause of blood disorders like hairy cell leukemia. It's a rare form of leukemia that could be genetic. The good news is that we can treat it with chemotherapy and possibly the surgical removal of your spleen," he replied.

Now, I was speechless. In disbelief that I could be diagnosed with cancer at thirty-four years of age, I reminded myself to breathe. My stomach knotted up, and I felt as if I could run my truck off the road into the ditch. Eventually, after listening to him speak for a minute or so more, not really processing much more of what he was saying, I asked, "Well, what are my chances of survival?"

There was a moment of silence, and then he replied, "Well, should you choose to do chemotherapy, the outlook is promising. Close to 90 percent of patients experience almost full remission up to five to ten years. Some even have longer remission rates up to fifteen years."

"So, should I undergo this treatment, is it likely that the cancer will come back?" I asked.

"Yes, we have no absolute cure for this disease, only a way to subdue the disease for a period of time. In some cases, the cancer never comes back."

I gulped. I could not believe I had an incurable disease. Sure, it sounded like my chances for survival were high, but what about the 10 percent who did not go into remission? Did they die? I didn't ask that at this moment. I could not bear to hear the answer. The thought of your own impending mortality being thrust upon you in the middle of an ordinary workday was preposterous, if not downright surreal. I hung up the phone, called my wife, and gave her the news. I had already pulled off the road at a gas station. Catherine, as always, sounded calm and composed, trying to be strong for me in the face of great adversity. I canceled my other sales calls and drove home in somber disbelief.

I paced the downstairs hallway of our new home as I waited for my wife to get home from work. When she finally arrived, we embraced and calculated what the next few months would look like. At this time, my wife was about two months pregnant with our first child. She followed up with my doctor and was reassured that the cancer had a high remission rate and that we needed to come in as soon as possible to figure out the best treatment regimen. That evening, I received a call from a hairy cell leukemia survivor from our church. He had been through the treatment several years ago and had been in remission for several years. He reassured me that this is one of the more treatable leukemias—in other words, it was not as deadly as some of the other more acute and chronic leukemias out there. While his call was reassuring and uplifting, I felt paralyzed by fear nonetheless. After all, this man had been much older when he had been diagnosed, as are the majority of people who get this kind of cancer. In fact, at thirty-four years of age, I was one of the youngest people to ever be diagnosed with it. That was sobering. Since so many people usually got diagnosed with this kind of leukemia later in life, the remission rates and cure rates were skewed. In fact, later that week, my doctor explained that oftentimes, older people go into remission from the disease for five to ten years but then die of other causes, so it's hard to say how long the cancer will remain in remission, if, in fact, I did go into remission. "At your age, it's highly likely that you will have to be treated more than once for this disease."

My next question was obvious: "What is the likelihood of not surviving the chemotherapy?"

"Well, there is a risk," he said. "Essentially, we will be completely depleting your immune system by eliminating nearly all your white blood cells. And we will need to watch your hemoglobin. If the hemoglobin gets too low, we may have to do a blood transfusion." Hemoglobin (Hb or Hgb) is a protein in red blood cells that carries oxygen throughout the body. He continued, "In essence, you will be at a high risk of contracting a bacterial infection or other type of infection, so we will keep you in the hospital for a week to treat you, monitor you, and watch your levels."

I was appalled at the idea of being in a hospital bed for a week—that seemed like an eternity. The doctor indicated that immediate treatment was not absolutely necessary but recommended. He knew that we might want to wait until after the baby was born. "Your HCL has been developing for many years now and is a very slow-developing disease. You are not in danger of dying in the near future, but we would want to treat this in the next year for sure. "

Catherine and I did not hesitate. She looked at me and then at the doctor. "I think we want to do this as soon as possible, and possibly be on the other side of this before the baby comes." The doctor agreed, and I was set up to begin treatment on November 1, 2015. I would be out of work for a month or more, depending on how well I did recovering from the chemotherapy. I would need to be quarantined with no visitors and no outside contact with the world for about a month until my white blood cells could build back to normal levels. If I did go out, I needed to wear a mask to avoid coming into contact with any airborne diseases.

My wife and I arrived at the hospital early on the morning of November 1, and we waited. Paperwork had to be assigned, my chemotherapy had to be repaired, and a PICC line needed to be inserted into my arm. A PICC is a long, thin tube called a catheter that goes into the body through a vein in the upper arm. The end of this catheter goes into a large vein near the heart. It was uncomfortable at first, but I did not even feel the line running through my body even though it was a tube that ran through my arm and down into my chest cavity. This would be the line that infused the chemo meds gradually over the course of the next seven days. For at least seven days, I would be attached to this line and the monitor, with nowhere to go but the hospital room itself, and occasionally the long, languid corridor that housed so many other cancer patients such as myself. As I lay there, I questioned my decision to do the chemotherapy, having no idea what to expect. Not only would I soon be neutropenic—devoid of white blood cells and platelets alike—I would more than likely feel physically deteriorated, nauseated, and extremely fatigued. When I asked my doctor how I would feel, he said, "I'm not going to lie; you are probably going to hate me. You will feel pretty bad for some time."

Finally, the chemo bag was attached to my PICC line, and the arduous journey began. My wife stayed for a few hours and then left to return the next day. Then, I was alone—just me and the chemo. When I spoke with Jason about this disease, he recommended I do my research and ask how many survivors there were of the medically prescribed chemotherapy. It turns out that, in this rare case, there is an 85 to 90 percent survival rate, depending on the type of chemo drug used. He said I should look into the Burzynski Clinic and change my diet, but as I did my research, I found that blood cancers are very different from tumorous cancers, and in my case, chemotherapy, although dangerous because of its poisonous effect on the body, was highly effective in the long run. As I lay there watching the poison drip slowly into my body, I began to second-guess myself. *What if I have made the wrong decision? After all, the doctor did say there was a small chance I would die from the treatment, either because of contracting a deadly disease or from low hemoglobin.*

I leaned over and read the medicine information on the IV bag. My doctor had chosen cladribine, and just below the description, it read "antineoplastic." It turns out that cladribine does, in fact, contain antineoplastics. Immediately, I felt that this was God's divine providence. Antineoplastics are quite different from antineoplastons, but the similarity gave me a thread of hope, while perhaps naïve and misguided, early on that God had a plan for this. (Cladribine belongs to the group of cancer-fighting medications known as antineoplastics and specifically to the group of antineoplastics known as antimetabolites. According to www.uniprix.com, cladribine is used specifically to treat hairy cell leukemia. Cladribine fights cancer by preventing the growth of cancer cells, which eventually results in their destruction.)

For the first few days of the treatment, I was very active. I finished three books and spent a lot of time out of bed—walking up and down the long, disease-infested corridor three or four times a day. I trudged painstakingly with my IV bag and cart attached down into the lobby, past the cafes, and even out the main entry a few times. One day, I even walked outside to get some fresh air. This was not a common occurrence, and I got some strange looks as I wandered around the hospital with a mask on my face and an IV bag attached. Some people frowned as if they felt sorry for such a young, strong-looking man in such a pathetic state. Keep in mind that I am six feet and one inch tall, weigh two hundred and twenty pounds, and appear pretty healthy to the average person. To see such a sight tiptoeing through a hallway with a mask and an IV bag and cart attached had to seem decidedly ironic to some people. And it's not like a lot of people did this. Most patients stayed in their rooms all day; at most they might walk the hallways in their wings. I, however, was heeding Jason's advice and getting as much as exercise as I could. He visited me one day in the hospital and said, "You need to be walking the halls four or five times a day for a half hour each. You need to keep your blood flowing, your body active, and your spirits up." Who would not heed the advice of a brain cancer survivor?

In fact, I had several visitors over the course of the eight days I spent in that room. Several people from my church came, guys from work visited, and of course my mother and father visited a couple of times. Everyone was always cheerful, although it was clear by the looks on their faces that they were appalled to see me laid up in a hospital bed with a pale, disheveled appearance. One visitor even got to witness one of the many bloody noses that I experienced. As the chemo annihilated my white and red blood cells and platelets, I was more inclined to bleeding as my body no longer had the platelets needed to stave off nosebleeds and the like. I also had to be very careful not to cut myself, as it would be difficult to stop the bleeding if I did.

After about three days of treatment, I lost my appetite completely and became inescapably fatigued. I found it very difficult to wake up in the mornings, and when I did, I had trouble keeping my eyes open. I was nauseated almost all of the time, and I began to even feel slightly feverish. The nurses would interrupt my sleep throughout the night to check my IV bag, draw blood, and check my vital signs. Essentially, they were drawing blood twice a day to check all my levels, including white blood count, red blood count, platelets, and hemoglobin. And when the IV bag ran low, the monitor would beep extremely loudly, waking me up repeatedly. There truly is no rest for the weary in a hospital room. There are always doctors, nurses, and other people coming in to perform their duties, not to mention janitors, hospital staff, and visitors going in and out. Although I was extremely tired, I do not think I ever slept more than three hours at a time, which of course added to this miserable feeling of ambient fatigue. My body was weakening, even slowly dying alongside the cancer. As the cladribine eradicated the cancer cells that invaded my body, it was also attacking and killing all the vital, healthy cells that a body requires to live. It was a sobering and frightening thought. I woke up with night sweats over the course of several nights in the hospital, and as I felt the pillow behind my head, it was cold and wet. I had bad dreams, and I thought I heard sinister voices telling me that I was sure to die before my child was born. Catherine would come in to visit the next day, and I looked at her belly growing bigger, carrying our child inside her; I began to feel a great sense of dread at being a daddy who would not be there for his child. Catherine, for her part, stayed positive for me. And up until the third day, she would bring me good food from several restaurants. After that, I had no desire to eat. There were several days in a row when all I had to eat was two spoons of applesauce and water. I heeded Jason's advice, though, and even when I felt absolutely miserable—malnourished, exhausted, and weakened by the poison in my veins—I got up and walked and walked. Even if I feigned vitality and strength, I was telling myself that I was still strong enough to walk around. I had to fight the cancer alongside the poisonous chemotherapy.

As the seventh day arrived, I was ready to go home. I was tired and sick, and I just wanted to be somewhere familiar. This stale and synthetic hospital room began to make me feel claustrophobic. My anxiety had increased tenfold, and I became restless in spite of the acute fatigue I was experiencing. Moreover, my nausea increased as my appetite diminished to not even a desire for water. I remember Dr. Escobar telling me that my hemoglobin was on the threshold of being dangerously low and I had officially reached a neutropenic state, with extremely low white blood cells, red blood cells, and platelets. Jason warned me against getting a blood transfusion, saying the risks were always high in doing so. While infectious diseases were not transferred from one patient to another at the same high rate as twenty years earlier, there was always the risk of a patient rejecting someone else's blood, so transfusions should only be used as a last alternative. Jason brought me sublingual B12 to help elevate my hemoglobin, and I was greatly appreciative.

I asked if I could go home at the end of the seventh day. My chemo regimen was scheduled to be completed the next morning, and the doctor said they would monitor my hemoglobin levels and let me know in the morning. If I did go home, I was to have no visitors at the house, and my wife and I should always wear masks around each other. Dr. Escobar said, "Look, Kyle, if you contract sepsis in your neutropenic state, you could die in an hour." He was not just saying this to shock me; he was telling me this so I would not refrain from returning to the dreaded hospital should I start to get a fever. "If you get a temperature at or above 100.4 degrees, you need to get back here immediately. We are putting you on antibiotics at home, but you need to get those antibiotics intravenously if you start to get a temperature." I agreed, being secretly certain that nothing, not even the arrival of death itself, could bring me back to this formidable and hateful room. I was close to going out of my mind from being in one room for eight days, on the verge of vomiting out my sleeplessness.

I had the nurse roll me out to the curb to get into my wife's car. I could barely stand up, and I am not exaggerating here. I had never in my life felt this kind of lifeless and bedraggled misery. It is hard to describe how bad I felt and how much I just wanted to get home. This feeling I had was one of absolute, insatiable fatigue that penetrated each and every part of my body, from my fingers and toes to the inside of my head, where I felt a slow, dull pounding that seemingly was working to be more noticeable than the nausea the ebbed and flowed with movement and time. As we drove home, my wife looked at me with an impermeable dread. What I did not know at the time was she was afraid. At the hospital, she felt I was well taken care of, but at home, she would now be the primary caretaker. I had begged her to get me out of there that day and had harassed the doctor and nurse practitioner to the point that they were probably glad to get rid of me.

As we arrived home, I barely made it up to the spare bedroom, where it was decided I would sleep. I was so miserable that I could barely open my eyes, and when I closed my eyes, the pounding in my head became more and more salient while the nausea became more impossible to ignore. In the middle of the night, I woke up in a panic and puked all over the side of the bed, prompting my wife to come rushing in to assist me in cleaning up the mess. Normally, whenever I threw up in the past, I felt better, but not now. I felt worse as I watched my poor wife of only five years humble herself to clean up my puke and prop me up in bed. I felt close to death now as my fever began to spike and cold night sweats persisted on and off throughout the night.

I was home for just under forty-eight hours when Catherine took my temperature, and it was clear that at 100.4 degrees I needed to go back to the hospital. She practically dragged me back to the place, and as Dr. Escobar entered the room, I looked at him and remembered his telling me a couple months back how much I would hate him. Now, I hated him for sure. I looked at him and asked him how long I would be there. He said, "Probably five days." Now, I was ready to strangle him. How would I make it another five days in this awful, compressed, and nihilistic environment? It was nothing against hospitals and doctors—they were just trying to save my life, after all. It was the feeling of shame and helplessness, as a thirty-four-year-old man trapped in a room, trying to weave my way through hours and hours of meaninglessness as life went on for everyone else on the outside. I felt weak and pathetic, and my wife needed a man—most of all a husband and a father. Instead, she had this guy, a puke machine who could barely move and was lying in bed all day, straining just to use the bathroom. I thought this only happened to old people, but suddenly I felt old before my time and on the verge of the unthinkable.

Over the next five days, the Lord began to speak to me in big ways. I began to feel that this cancer was his way of rescuing me from the sin that had plagued my spirit for some time. I had battled alcohol addiction for many years leading up to this diagnosis, and I resolved to give it up for good if I ever got out of that hospital. As I prayed, read the Bible, and listened for God's words amid the quiet, it finally occurred to me that God had plans for my life, and this battle with cancer was a prerequisite to begin transforming me into the man he wanted to be. In the twenty-ninth chapter of Jeremiah, verse eleven, God speaks to his prophet: "For I know the plans I have for you, plans for welfare and not for evil, to give you a future and a hope" (Jer. 29:11).

I was released from the hospital on November 16, 2015, fifteen years to the day after my good friend Miranda had died at just twenty years of age. It was also the same day that my grandfather would die just one year later and the day my mom was diagnosed with terminal cancer two years later. But God chose November 16 as a day that I would finally commit to dying to myself. For Christ says, "For whoever would save his life will lose it, but whoever loses his life for my sake will have it." God had shown mercy on me and was going to let me live. With the infection that had caused my fever to spike now eliminated, I would return home to quarantine to try to get well.

I had lost twenty pounds in those thirteen days of not eating much of anything, and I remember coming home from the hospital with an appetite for the first time in what seemed like many months. Catherine had purchased a ham sandwich for me at the hospital café, and I can still taste the juicy ham and melted cheese on a croissant as I savored it until the last bite. Everything looked different already. I felt so grateful to finally be home, having suffered through thirteen days in that hospital. Over the course of the next several weeks, my white blood cells regenerated, my platelets rose, and I began to feel better. I had to go every few days to the clinic to have my blood levels checked, and praise God Almighty, my hemoglobin began to rise along with the other vital cells. However, I was not in remission yet. Another delightful biopsy was to come in just a couple of months to determine if the hairy leukemia cells had been eliminated.

At home over the next month, I did a lot of reading, and I began writing this book. I felt God had lit a spark in me to be a part of his new creation, letting the old, sinful self begin to slowly pass away.

When I returned to the doctor a couple of weeks later, Catherine and I asked how he had been, and he said, "You're not going to believe this, but I was hospitalized a week ago."

"For what?" we asked.

He replied, "I had sepsis."

We looked at him in disbelief, wondering how he was doing now. "Was that not the same thing you warned me about contracting when I was neutropenic?"

"Yes," he said. "Glad I got it and not you. I am doing fine now."

To this day, I am convinced that the Lord was showing me how very close to death I had been. Dr. Escobar had contracted sepsis in my place, just as Christ had died in my place on the cross. Perhaps

Dr. Escobar even got the disease while he was in the hospital room with me just a couple of weeks earlier and I somehow was spared. Those words rang in my ears: "If you get sepsis, you'll be dead in an hour."

We serve a merciful and loving God—a God who uses suffering and despair to draw people closer to him. It is only in discovering how meaningless life is without God that people can truly appreciate what a wonderful and mighty Creator we have, who supplies our every need on this earth. Just one month later, I was declared to be in remission from hairy cell leukemia, just a week or two before our beautiful daughter was born. We named her Annelise, which means "blessed (or graced) by God's promise." Two weeks prior to my chemotherapy treatment, the Lord had come to me in a dream and showed me through his mighty Word that I would be healed of this disease. And the Lord, as always, kept his promise. But I wasn't just healed of cancer in that hospital; I was cured of my old, iniquitous ways. When temptation to behave as I did in the past comes my way now, I think back to my time with God in that hospital, where he saved me from myself. He took my hand and guided me out on November 16, 2015, saying, "Today is a day of renewal and transformation." I remembered that my grandfather went home to the Lord on the very same day a year later, and again the next year, when my mom died just nine days after being declared terminal on November 16. People say God works in mysterious ways, but they are really not as mysterious as we like to sometimes suppose they are. For God's ways have been revealed to those who believe in Jesus Christ. Our God is a God of infinite love, grace, hope, and wisdom. He would do anything to save us from the Devil, death, and disease. And that is why he came to die on a cross— to be crucified in order to rescue us from the sin that obliterates and destroys the very soul that God intended to live and live abundantly.

Works Cited

Beat Cancer Organization, copyright 2018, https://www.beatcancer.org

Burzynski Clinic, copyright 2006-2013, http://www.burzynskiclinic.com

Burzynski Patient Group, copyright 2011, http://www.burzynskipatient group.org/

Carson, Ben. *Think Big*, DefaultBrand; 33815th edition, 1994.

"Chief Okemos in Life and Death," accessed December 2015 at http://geo.msu.edu/extra/geogmich/okemosgrave.html

Cure Your Own Cancer Organization, copyright 2011-2018, http://www.cureyourowncancer.org.

Eldredge, John. *Wild at Heart*, Nashville, Tennessee, Thomas Nelson, 2001, 2010.

"Mental Confusion or Delirium," Cancer.net, accessed June 2016, https://www.cancer.net/navigating-cancer-care/side-effects/mental-confusion-or-delirium.

Metaxas, Eric, *Miracles*, New York: Plume, 2014.

CPSIA information can be obtained
at www.ICGtesting.com
Printed in the USA
BVHW081022020919
557347BV00007BA/40/P